Where Are the Elephants?

Leon Rosselson

D0168791

Where Are the Elephants?
Leon Rosselson
This edition © 2023 PM Press

ISBN: 978-1-62963-973-4 (paperback)
ISBN: 978-1-62963-988-8 (ebook)
Library of Congress Control Number: 2022931969

Cover by John Yates / www.stealworks.com
Cover photo courtesy Sharon Latham / www.sharonsprints.com
Interior design by briandesign

10 9 8 7 6 5 4 3 2 1

PM Press
PO Box 23912
Oakland, CA 94623
www.pmpress.org

Printed in the USA

'In many ways, Leon Rosselson is the embodiment of the original ideals of punk rock. His hair isn't spiky, but his music is, using fearless wit and political integrity to highlight the hypocrisies of those in power. Alone among the great British songwriters of the past sixty years, Leon has sought to make art that stays true to Karl Marx's demand that we should concern ourselves with the ruthless criticism of all that exists.'
—**Billy Bragg**

'Rosselson remains fearless. He provides something that the world is in dire need of currently—dissent that seeks dialogue versus greater division and disconnection.'
—**Ian Brennan, Grammy-winning music producer and author, *Silenced by Sound* and *Muse-Sick: a music meritocracy in fifty-nine notes***

'Leon Rosselson's *Where Are the Elephants?* is a fascinating mixture of autobiography, critical inquiry, and polemic, spanning his long life as a musician, author, and revolutionary. Rosselson's rich experience is the basis for profound insights on many themes central to an appraisal of the 20th century and the beginning of the 21st. From folk music and songwriting to communism and anti-semitism, from protest and demonstration to rancorous political debate, Rosselson weighs in, not as an observer, but as a participant. His is the testimony of an engaged artist dedicated to his craft and the struggle against suffering and injustice. Anyone interested in music, England, Jewish identity in opposition to Zionism, critical takes on Bob Dylan and Leonard Cohen, or Jesus and Judas Iscariot, this book is for you. And lest it be forgotten in the breadth of its subject matter, *Where Are the Elephants?* is exemplary as autobiography: the sharing of a full life with grace and humility.'
—**Mat Callahan, musician and author of *Working-Class Heroes: A History of Struggle in Song***

My thanks to all those who have supported and contributed to my songwriting life and in particular to Frankie Armstrong, Roy Bailey, Billy Bragg, Martin Carthy, Chris Foster, Robb Johnson, Ramsey Kanaan, Reem Kelani, Nancy Kerr, Sandra Kerr, Elizabeth Mansfield, Marisa Orth-Pallavicini, Rina Rosselson, Janet Russell, Ian Saville, Fiz Shapur.

For Rina, with love

True, I don't wear my heart upon my sleeve
(which doesn't mean, of course, I haven't got one).
And though I have my faults (so you believe)
emotional incontinence is not one.
My love for you I may not always show
(which doesn't mean to say that I don't feel it).
And sometimes I cause hurt and then I'm slow
to find my way to the words I need to heal it.
And, as for hugs, you'll doubt it but I mean
to give you two a day at least. And yet
I know they are too few and far between.
Despite my best intentions, I forget.
But still, please note, for this is also true
I've penned this heartfelt sonnet just for you.

Contents

1   Communism, or Where Are the Elephants?   1

2   The Power of Song   53

3   Stand Up, Stand Up for Song   59

4   Me, Georges Brassens, and the Last Chance   64

5   Sing a Song of Politics   74

6   Stand Up for Judas   81

7   Beware! It Is Catching and Can Rot Your Brain   90

8   Welcome to the Witch Hunt   92

9   Theodor Herzl: Visionary or Antisemite?   100

10   Israel and the Labour Party: A Love Story   109

11   My Life as a Songwriter (or How I Failed to Become
     Rich and Famous) in Twenty-Three Episodes   119

12   Coronavirus: March 2020   133

13   Stay-at-Home Days   137

14   Interview with Robb Johnson   138

     INDEX   163

     ABOUT THE AUTHORS   170

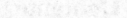

Communism, or Where Are the Elephants?

'The most radical humanist vision that ever existed … communism promised to wipe out every form of exploitation, oppression, discrimination and violence.'

—Michael Brie

'Men fight and lose the battle, and the thing that they fought for comes about in spite of their defeat, and when it comes it turns out not to be what they meant, and other men have to fight for what they meant under another name.'

—William Morris

'A map of the world that does not include Utopia is not worth even glancing at, for it leaves out the one country at which Humanity is always landing. And when it lands there, it looks out, and, seeing a better country, sets sail. Progress is the realization of Utopias.'

—Oscar Wilde

As I remember it, on the morning of my seventh birthday, 22 June 1941, my father opened the door of our flat in Tufnell Park to the Co-op milkman who delivered the usual pint bottle of milk together with the news that Nazi Germany had attacked the Soviet Union. Operation Barbarossa. At first, my father refused to believe it. I didn't understand why. I suppose, as a devout follower of the Soviet Union, he could not admit to himself that Stalin might have made a mistake in assuming that the Molotov-Ribbentrop Non-Aggression Pact, which, of course, my father supported, would protect the Soviet Union from a German attack. When the news was confirmed, he declared that this signaled the end for Hitler's Germany. He had no doubts at all. Communism was unvanquishable.

At that time we couldn't read our family's newspaper of choice, the Communist *Daily Worker*, because it had been banned for following the Comintern line that the war should be opposed as an imperialist war. Some in the leadership of the Communist Party were appalled by this decision, notably Harry Pollitt whose name I often heard bandied about in discussions and arguments at home. Now, with the attack on the Soviet Union, the CP decreed that overnight the war had become a people's war and members were urged to support it without reservation.

I spent much of those childhood years, when I wasn't being evacuated, hovering over the wireless at home, listening to the BBC news and plotting the course of the battles on the Eastern Front. During those terrible early months of defeat and retreat when it looked certain that the Soviet Army would be overrun, my father's confidence never seemed to waver. These were tactical retreats, luring the enemy to their doom. In my memory, my mother's main contribution to the family discussions was to swear at Hitler and his Nazis in Yiddish.

Then came the Nazis' failure to take Leningrad, followed by the failure of its offensive against Moscow.

The *Daily Worker* was, to great rejoicing in our house, unbanned in September 1942 so we no longer had to rely on the capitalist BBC for our news. And we could read, day after day, month after month, our paper's extraordinary reports on the Battle of Stalingrad, the courage, the heroism, the sacrifices of the ordinary Russian soldiers, and the ultimate crushing defeat of Hitler's invaders. The Red Army—our

Red Army—had prevailed, just as my father had predicted. This was the turning point of the war, as even the capitalist press and Winston Churchill had to acknowledge, for we were no longer alone in our admiration for Soviet Russia and its heroic army.

It's difficult to fully appreciate even now the terrible losses, the appalling destruction suffered by Russia in the war. Some twenty-five million dead and a country laid waste. At the time, I think I was too agitated, too excited by reading and hearing about the battles and the defeats and the victories to be upset by the slaughter and the suffering.

My parents, as far as I can remember, never told me what to think or what I should believe. But then, of course, they didn't need to. Fuzzy images from my growing-up life still linger in my brain: a small girl hands a bouquet of flowers to a smiling Uncle Joe; happy peasant women sing as they march off to reap the golden wheat fields; a heroic Stakhanovite worker, glowing with pride, bears aloft the red flag; a group of red-scarved Komsomol children gaze into a radiant future.

And then there were the songs. I can still sing them, though the lyrics may have fragmented a bit. That old Russian Civil War song, revived in the war against Nazi Germany:

> With Budyonny to lead us for the cause that had freed us
> We swept forward by night and by day.
> Soon our fame rode before us like a thundering chorus
> As the army that never gave way.

Many of those old Bolshevik military leaders had been murdered by Stalin in the purges of the 1930s, but I didn't know that then.

I was beguiled by *Salute to Life*, with an uplifting tune by Shostakovich:

> The wind has a breath of the morning
> Then meet it with banners unfurled.

3

Let joy be your clarion, comrade,
We march in the dawn of the world.
Then, comrades, face the wind, salute
The rising sun.
Our country turns towards the dawn
New life's begun.

How could I resist that vision of a glorious future?

To complete my education, I was given books that no school friend of mine had ever read. Red diaper babies, as they're called in the United States, would have been fed a diet of Howard Fast's children's books. The English equivalent was Geoffrey Trease. I was thrilled by *Bows against the Barons*, a Marxist version of the Robin Hood story, in which Robin's vision of 'an England without masters' is betrayed, but, as Little John says, 'we'll go on working to make Robin's dream come true.' In *Missing from Home*, a teenage brother and sister run away from their middle-class home and learn about the class war by helping factory workers win a strike. *Red Comet*—two English children visit the happy wonderland of the Soviet Union in the 1930s—was somewhat lifeless and too didactic for my tastes but I liked a book called *Eddie and the Gypsy*, by a German writer, which explained Marx's theory of surplus value by way of fishing and who owns the catch. Apart from *Eddie and the Gypsy*, which sadly I lost somewhere, I still have these books, somewhat tattered now but so evocative of my growing-up time.

Was I being brainwashed? No more so than any other boy or girl who attended school, Cubs, Scouts, church, synagogue, or Girl Guides and read comics and Biggles books. I was absorbing ideas and a certain narrative: that the way the world was set up was unfair; that some had too much and others too little; that the powerful made the rules to benefit themselves; that we were Jews and so should always be on the side of the oppressed; and that somewhere over the rainbow there was a sunlit land 'so dear to every toiler,' as the song said, where life was lived differently, where all had equal worth and led lives of peace, harmony, and comradeship. In short, I was being enlisted in the ranks of the Opposition to What Is.

Our Jewishness centred on food rather than religion. My mother, brought up in the Jewish East End of London, cooked the traditional Ashkenazi dishes to accompany the Jewish festivals and sent me to school with sandwiches made with what she called 'gribenes' (schmaltz and fried onions), which, she assured me, would keep me warm in the cold winter months. They, along with my mother's homemade hamantaschen, were my favourites.

In the run-up to the election of 1950, the headmaster of my school, an all-boys grammar situated on the edge of Parliament Hill and Hampstead Heath, announced that the school would be holding a mock election while the real election was taking place. This, he said, would be an education in how democracy works. By this time, the Communist Party was thoroughly disillusioned with Attlee's Labour government, attacking it for its austerity and anti-strike policies, its rearmament programme, its anti-Soviet Cold War stance, its anti-Communist purges, its decision to ally Britain with the United States and NATO. So, partly as a provocation but also because all the political parties except for the Communist Party were represented, I decided, in the interests of democracy, to nominate myself as the Communist candidate. The reaction was swift. On the headmaster's orders, I was banned. My name was removed from the list. That was my first lesson in democracy.

I was never given an explanation. I think the fear was that, boys being boys and instinctively anti-authoritarian and snook-cocking, I might win the election and the *Daily Mirror* might get wind of it and, in the context of the anti-Soviet, anti-Communist scare campaign, a hollow echo of the hysterical red-baiting infecting America, that would be a stain on the honour of the school.

I don't remember the result of the school election, but in the real election, Labour won with a much-reduced majority. The following year, they were voted out of office. We then had thirteen years of Tory rule. So much for the Parliamentary Road to Socialism.

The Cold War jitterbug was now in full swing. It was time to take sides. There were the peace-loving socialist countries on one side of the Iron Curtain and war-mongering America and its acolytes on the other. Or there was totalitarian communism on one side and the free world on the other. Peace or freedom. Take your choice. We—communists and fellow travellers—lined up behind the peace banner. 'Ain't gonna study war no more,' we sang. And: 'A mighty song of peace will soon be ringing.' We felt betrayed by the Labour Party's decision to develop the nuclear bomb—one 'with the bloody Union Jack on top of it,' as Ernest Bevin so delicately phrased it. This made us a prime target in any future nuclear war. Peaceful coexistence was the imperative. In the words of Vern Partlow's 'Old Man Atom':

> If you're scared of the A-bomb, I'll tell you what to do
> You got to get with all the people in the world with you
> You got to get together and let out a yell
> Or the first thing you know we'll blow this world to …

It wasn't that I was opposed to freedom, but what was the point of freedom if we were all going to be incinerated? And what sort of freedom was it, anyway, that murdered Ethel and Julius Rosenberg?

Sporting events also required us to take sides. Emil Zatopek's triple gold in the Helsinki Olympic Games of 1952 was a thrilling achievement but doubly thrilling in that he represented what a small country could achieve under socialism. And when my home team, Arsenal, lost 5–0 to

Moscow Dynamo in a friendly match, it was surely a sign that communist football was the future.

We had to cope with and combat daily attacks on the Soviet Union and its allies by the capitalist press. More disturbing were the ugly rumours swirling around about antisemitism in the Soviet Union. Some were asking about Mikhoels and the celebrated Moscow State Yiddish Theatre company. What had happened to them? My father was having none of it. After all, hadn't the Soviet Union instituted the first Jewish autonomous territory? It was called Birobidzhan, national language Yiddish, and it had given us a song, something about a Jewish collective farm, with a jolly chorus: *Hey Zhan, hey Zhankoye, hey Zhanvili, hey Zhankoye.* In the 1960s, everyone from Pete Seeger to the Limeliters was singing it, though the heyday of this Jewish entity with its collective farms and women tractor drivers was long gone.

Then there was the Slánský trial in Czechoslovakia. Thirteen Communist Party bureaucrats, ten of them Jewish, accused of a Zionist imperialist conspiracy. What were we to think? Most of my friends in Hashomer Hatzair dismissed the accusations as a fabrication. A few worried that they could be true, casting doubt on their Zionist beliefs. The Doctors' Plot was another unpleasant pill to swallow, but, in the event, we needn't have swallowed it since it turned out, after Stalin's death in March 1953, to have been another fabrication.

So by November 1954, when, as a representative of the University Socialist Club (a Communist front organisation), I joined a youth delegation to the Soviet Union, my faith in the goodness of the Union of Soviet Socialist Republics was being tested. What's more, Wolverhampton Wanderers had just beaten Moscow Spartak 4–0, thus undermining my confidence in the superiority of communist football.

The delegation comprised a number of trade unionists, Quakers, students, Christians, one from the YCL (the Young

Communist League), a couple of Young Liberals, and at least one Tory. Most were in their mid to late twenties. I was the youngest. Some, especially the Young Liberals, came with their political prejudices on high alert, determined to find fault. Others were more open-minded, prepared to put their preconceived ideas on hold.

I decided to dump my doubts and prepared myself to defend the Soviet system against the inevitable criticisms and snide questions. Why are elderly ladies the only ones clearing the Moscow streets of snow? Why does everyone wear such drab clothes? Why, if this is a classless society, are there four classes in the trains? Why were some of the group detained by the militia for taking photos of decaying houses in the old part of Moscow? Since factory workers are on a piece-rate system, isn't there a conflict of interest between workers and management?

I had formulated two main lines of defence: that it was only nine years after a war that had devastated the country, destroyed its main cities, and killed over twenty million people; that, contrary to popular opinion, the Soviet Union did not claim to be a communist society. It was on the road to communism but passing through the socialist stage, expressed in the slogan 'From each according to his ability, to each according to his work.'

For the higher phase of communism, the slogan, coined by Marx, was 'From each according to his ability, to each according to his needs.' I hoped I'd remembered that correctly and could, if pushed, explain the difference. As for the expected attacks on Stalin as a ruthless dictator, I could reply that, if the Russians thought he had oppressed them, they showed it in a strange way by queuing outside his tomb to pay homage to him.

Accompanied by our student interpreter guides (doubt-less spying for the secret service, asserted the Young Liberals), we visited Moscow, Leningrad, Georgia, the Bolshoi, the

Metro, the Kremlin, the Lenin Library, the Lenin Mausoleum, St. Basil's Church, a coke and gas plant, a champagne factory, Rustavi Metallurgical Plant, universities, an orphanage, the Anti-Fascist Committee of Soviet Youth, a Pioneer Palace, and Tbilisi football stadium. We were fed a mass of instantly forgettable statistics and drank endless toasts to 'mir i druzhba' (or, for a change, 'druzhba i mir') which, in Georgia, started at breakfast and ended with half the delegation in a state of confused inebriation.

In Moscow, I went with Raya, one of our interpreters, to visit a branch of my father's family, the only other Rosselsons that I know of. My father had a half-brother, born from his mother's previous marriage. She had, so the story goes, divorced that husband for smoking on the sabbath. As an only son, he was exempt from serving in the tsar's army. When my father was born, his mother did not register the birth so that the half-brother would not be called up into the army. So my father had no papers and no future. Legally he did not exist, which is why, when he was fourteen, his mother took him to England to live with his uncle, Rabbi Newman, in Leicester.

The Moscow Rosselsons—father, mother, two sons aged eight and sixteen—lived in a dingy block of flats in the old part of the city, a back street near the Red Square. The flat itself, though small, was warm and comfortable and well-furnished. It was a strange meeting. Since I had given them no warning, they never quite recovered from the shock of finding a new relative. It occurred to me afterwards that in this unsettled struggle-for-power period between the death of Stalin and Khrushchev's 1956 de-Stalinisation speech, they may well have been wary of talking to a foreigner, a Westerner, especially one accompanied by an official interpreter.

I don't remember what we talked about. Not politics, for sure. Football probably. I remember the younger boy played something on the piano.

Sometime in the 1980s, like thousands of other Soviet Jews, the younger son, with his wife, mother, and two daughters, applied to emigrate to Israel. In transit in Vienna, like thousands of other Soviet Jews, they changed direction and were granted a visa for the United States. When I was touring the States in 1990, I visited the family in Chicago. The two teenage daughters were fully fledged Americans and ardent Reaganites. Their father lamented their rejection of their Russian background and culture.

My father's sister's family in Kiev also joined the mass emigration of Jews at that time. They ended up in Israel. To my father this was incomprehensible. In his contacts with them over the years, they had never given him the impression that they were unhappy in the Soviet Union, that they suffered from antisemitism. But it was more than a shock that his Russian family should leave their Soviet homeland for the capitalist West; it was, for him, a betrayal.

In 1953, influenced by my two YCL sisters, I joined the London Youth Choir, a left-wing choir which specialised in singing what could be described as political folk songs. We were not all communists, but we were certainly sympathetic to what we considered to be the socialist countries of the world and were highly critical of the United States, both its foreign policy and its anticommunist witch hunt—the blacklist, after all, harmed the careers of our favourite folksingers, Pete Seeger and the Weavers. We were also opposed to Britain's Bomb and its colonial wars in Malaya and Kenya. Most of all we didn't want to be turned into radioactive dust in a nuclear war.

We sang folk songs because the Communist Party espoused folk song as the music of the people (i.e., the working class) even though it wasn't. Folk song was indeed, as the House Un-American Activities Committee believed, a communist conspiracy. We sang political songs and peace songs that we found in *Sing* magazine, the equivalent of

Sing Out! in America. We sang carols in Trafalgar Square at Christmastime. We sang American songs and songs from around the world because we were internationalists. We sang in political meetings and in halls and in the streets and squares and markets of London to raise money for our trips to the World Festivals of Youth and to bring back our message of peaceful coexistence from those festivals. In John Hasted's words ('It Was When We Went to Moscow'): *Have you heard about the Festival in Poland far away? / It's the greatest celebration that there's been for many a day. / We are saving up our pennies and we're counting every stitch / And we're going to get to Warsaw even if we have to hitch.*

The World Youth Festivals, which ran every two years from 1947 in Prague to Moscow in 1957, were, according to its Cold War critics, a tool of Soviet diplomacy, a brainwashing exercise, a public relations extravaganza. For the choir, they were an opportunity to experience, however briefly and superficially, life behind the Iron Curtain, to meet young people from all over the world and listen to their songs and choirs and musicians and exchange badges and gifts. And we were happy to join in the anthem of the festivals, even though the somewhat platitudinous lyrics didn't quite ring true:

> *Everywhere the youth is singing freedom's song …*
> *We rejoice to show the world that we are strong …*
> *We are the youth*
> *and the world proclaims our song of truth.*

I went with the choir to the Bucharest Festival in 1953, Warsaw in 1955 and Moscow in 1957. Did I feel that I was being brainwashed? Apart from a school trip to Dieppe, Bucharest was the first time I'd ever left England's shores and I was too dazzled by all the very attractive young women from a myriad of different countries, often dressed in colourful traditional costumes, who were eager to talk with me and exchange messages of peace and friendship, to ask myself that question.

Warsaw was a darker experience. It had been destroyed in the war; ruined buildings still littered the streets; giant billboards displayed grim photos of Warsaw under the Nazi occupation. The obligatory visit to Auschwitz didn't exactly lighten the mood, and the Polish people themselves seemed downbeat, probably with some justification. Of course, historically Russia and Poland had not been the best of friends. The Soviet Union had donated to Warsaw a giant present, the Palace of Culture, for which its citizens were eternally ungrateful. The joke going round was that the best view of Warsaw was to be had from the Palace of Culture because it was the only place in the city from where you couldn't see the Palace of Culture.

Then came 1956. Khrushchev's speech, Hungary, Suez. I don't remember when exactly I read about Khrushchev's denunciation of the cult of personality and Stalin's crimes. I doubt I read the whole speech. I was, I suppose, shocked but not altogether surprised. By that time, the songs of the Soviet Union that had thrilled me in my childhood were beginning to sound discordant. Nothing rhymed any more. Unlike my two sisters, I had never joined the Young Communist League so I didn't have to make the agonising choice of whether to leave or stay. Thousands left.

And then in November, when Russian tanks invaded Hungary and the *Daily Worker* attacked the uprising as a fascist counterrevolution and sacked its foreign correspondent, Peter Fryer, because his reports were sympathetic to the demands of the workers and students who were being killed, thousands more resigned their party membership in disgust. The Communist Party was broken apart. I remember being in the demonstration in Trafalgar Square on 4 November listening to Bevan's passionate attack on Anthony Eden and Britain's invasion of Suez and feeling that these momentous events were changing the world.

Did Khrushchev's speech and the crushing of the Hungarian uprising cause my father to reassess his loyalty to the Soviet Union? If so, he never admitted it to me. He continued to read the *Daily Worker* and trust its political stance over the years and after it morphed into the *Morning Star* and over the decades until the day he died, just before 'actually existing socialism' and the pillars of the Soviet system collapsed.

In a sense, there was nowhere else for him to go. He had been brought up under the repressive rule of the tsar. He claimed that he could remember the pogroms of 1905. There were occasions when, since he had no papers, he had had to hide from the tsarist police. Then, when he was seventeen, three years after he had landed in England, the impossible had happened. The workers in the tsarist empire had risen up, overthrown the tsar, and taken power. A new world was born. He never knew his actual birth date so he chose one for himself: 7 November, the date of the Bolshevik revolution with its slogan: All Power to the Soviets. As the poet wrote of another revolution:

> *Bliss was it in that dawn to be alive*
> *But to be young was very heaven!*

For him, the Russian Revolution, led by Lenin and the Communist Party, was the great hope of the world. How could he abandon it?

You can't know what it meant and the pride that we felt to know working people, people like us / Could shake off the shackles, could topple the palaces, remake the world without ruler or boss, as the old Communist in my song expressed it.

Many of those who stayed in the party considered those who left as renegades. I have a vivid memory of a bus stop conversation with a woman I knew slightly who had remained loyal. Her anger at what she considered the betrayal of those who had deserted the cause shook me. It was visceral. It was personal. It was beyond arguments about ideology or politics. It was an emotional attachment—not to a party or to a country but to a vision, a vision of another better world that will be born, that must be born, where war, exploitation, injustice would be no more. To abandon that vision was to betray the future.

> *You may say we were duped, well, we paid for our dreams:*
> *   broken lives, broken marriages, jobs lost and jail*
> *Some lost heart and left, some betrayed us for medals,*
> *   there are always some turncoats whose souls are for*
> *   sale*
> *But the best of us never surrendered our vision, and we*
> *   kept the faith through the bleakest defeat.*
> *Do you think that was easy, surrounded by hatred, the*
> *   sneer of indifference, the hurt of deceit?*
> *And our lives were made rich by the cause that we fought*
> *   for, the friendship, the fellowship, sharing one aim*
> *To transform society, end exploitation—and that day will*
> *   come yet, though not in my time.*
> ('Song of the Old Communist')

This period of liberalisation when censorship was relaxed, political prisoners were released, and those unjustly executed by Stalin were rehabilitated was called the Thaw, after Ilya Ehrenburg's novel, and we welcomed it. We welcomed also Khrushchev's policy of peaceful coexistence as a way to reduce the tensions and threats of the Cold War and nuclear annihilation. So the World Youth Festival in Moscow in July 1957 took place at a far more propitious, optimistic time than the other two festivals I'd been to. I remember the opening ceremony with thousands of young people in colourful costumes pouring into the stadium as a joyous occasion. Even the anthem sounded less like a dull platitude and more like a bright promise.

One great vision unites us though remote be the lands of
  our birth
Foes may threaten and smite us, still we live to bring peace
  to the earth.

So I sang with the choir in the streets, played my guitar in concerts, had serious discussions with Russian youth, ate Russian ice cream, fell asleep at the Bolshoi during *Prince Igor* (or was it *Boris Godounov*?), had my photo taken with attractive young women in traditional dress, listened to concerts of world music before the term was invented. Music was everywhere.

Britain sent, God bless my soul!
Skiffle, jazz, and rock 'n' roll
Said Comrade Shepilov, man alive!
I don't dig this bourgeois jive
But Khrushchev, ah, now he's the man
Who wants more skiffle in the 5 Year Plan
And that's why Shepilov's been sent
To a washboard factory in Outer Tashkent.
See you later . . . deviator.
Now you may think that's neither here nor there
But May Day next you'll see, I swear
Massed skiffle groups in the old Red Square
Washboards gleaming row on row
Don't you purge me Daddy-o.

As my contribution to this 'Talking Moscow Blues' shows, I looked on the political infighting taking place at that time with an amused scepticism. And we were not naive about the way the Soviet authorities were using the Moscow festival to burnish the image of the Soviet Union in the world. But that's not how we experienced it. For us it was more like one big party. When young people gather in their thousands across the political divide, it is impossible to control how they communicate, where they go, who they meet, what ideas they exchange. What happened in Moscow was largely out of the control of the Communist Party apparatchiks.

And for a few years, as the Soviet Union continued to relax its bureaucratic control of the daily lives of its people, we lived in the hope that perhaps it would change sufficiently to offer a genuine socialist alternative to the capitalist society, based on profit, inequality, exploitation, and war, that we opposed. It never happened. Nor, I finally decided, could it have. When all the major decisions are taken by the upper echelons in the Communist Party, representing the state, and the reins of power are held by the first secretary of the party, genuine change from below becomes impossible. So, in time, the more flexible, somewhat emotional policies of Khrushchev gave way to the rigid rule of Brezhnev. And in the 1960s, when in the Western world all was in flux, the Soviet Union froze. The questions, though, remained: If not the Soviet Union, where? And if not communism, what?

I was, nevertheless, glad the Soviet Union existed if only as a counterweight to the lumbering giant that was the American Empire, bullying and bribing its way around the globe, fixing elections in its sphere of influence, bringing down governments resistant to its embrace, installing dictators ready to do its bidding. When Castro's guerrilla army overthrew Batista's Mafia regime in 1958 and then started nationalising US property and assets and the Eisenhower administration imposed a tight embargo, I was thankful that the Soviet Union was there to support the Cuban Revolution, which could not otherwise have survived. What I hadn't bargained for was that, as a result of this Cold War confrontation, the world would soon teeter on the edge of a nuclear war.

I have a photo of myself playing the accordion on the first Campaign for Nuclear Disarmament (CND) march to Aldermaston in Easter 1958. It was, I remember, a most musical march—songs, jazz bands, choirs, including the London

Youth Choir. It was the first time I had experienced the heartening, elevating effect of singing together on a protest demonstration. It was a long walk, though I'm sure I dropped out before the end of the four days. There had been a meeting of the *Sing* magazine committee to decide on the anthem for the march. The choice was John Brunner's 'H Bombs Thunder,' set to the easy-to-sing tune of 'Miner's Lifeguard.'

> *Don't you hear the H-Bombs' thunder*
> *Echo like the crack of doom?*

It was an inspired choice. The straightforward chorus turned out to be eminently singable, and the song has probably been the most long-lasting of all those antinuclear songs written at that time.

> *Men and women, stand together*
> *Do not heed the men of war*
> *Make your minds up now or never*
> *Ban the Bomb for evermore.*

The irony is that the CND organisers wanted a silent march. Four days of silent walking would have been unbearable. It was a lesson learned.

We wanted a world free of nuclear weapons but the focus of the campaign was Britain's so-called independent nuclear deterrent, which was neither independent nor a deterrent. It could not be used without America's agreement and made us a prime target in the event of a nuclear war. And it increased the risks of an accidental conflagration. Sometime in the early 1960s, the Conservative government issued a booklet called *Civil Defence Instructions*. I used to have a copy. It offered advice to householders on how to survive a nuclear war and began with this comforting thought: 'If the bomb drops, organised help will be available.' Its advice was so patently absurd it must have brought thousands more into the campaign against the Bomb.

WHERE ARE THE ELEPHANTS?

Don't cower like a shower when the clouds begin to loom
Stand firm! Stand firm!
You will have a good four minutes to prepare your refuge
room
Stand firm! Stand firm!
For our Early Warning System will be broadcasting the
news
So don't sprawl around Trafalgar Square or lounge about
the loos
And switch off all electric fires so's not to blow a fuse
Stand firm! Stand firm!
A slit trench will protect you from the fallout and the blast
Stand firm! Stand firm!
And don't emerge from hiding while the radiation lasts
Stand firm! Stand firm!
To prove to the aggressor that free men will be free
Crouch down in your hidey-holes, make lots of pots of tea
If you're caught out in the open, duck behind a tree
And Stand firm! Stand firm!
('Stand Firm')

The Communist Party had its own front organisation, the British Peace Committee, but it could not compete with the appeal of the non-aligned CND which brought together Communists, particularly YCL members (though some in the party had reservations), Labour Party members, trade unionists, Christians, Quakers, the New Left, students, and others with no party affiliations. CND marches to and from Aldermaston became a regular Easter pilgrimage, gathering more and more people each year. In 1963, one hundred thousand protesters surged into Trafalgar Square at the end of the march. The previous October the world had come terrifyingly close to an insane nuclear conflagration: the Cuban Missile Crisis. It was an eerie moment. I remember being on the one hand terrified that this was it, this would be the catastrophe we had warned against, and on the other hand somehow sure that the two superpowers would not be so stupid as to embark on a war that would threaten the continuation of life on the planet.

> *Across the hills, black clouds are sweeping*
> *Carry poison far and wide*
> *And the grass has blackened underfoot*
> *And the rose has withered and died.*

> *But the rose is still as red, love, and the grass is still as*
>   *green*
> *And it must have been a shadow in the distance you have*
>   *seen*
> *Yes, it must have been a shadow you have seen.*

> *But can't you see the white ash falling*
> *From the hollow of the skies?*
> *And the blood runs red down the blackened walls*
> *Where a ruined city lies.*

> *I can see the red sun shining in the park on the stream*
> *And you must have felt a shiver from the darkness of a*
>   *dream*
> *Yes, it must have been the darkness of a dream.*
> ('Across the Hills')

As we learned afterwards, nuclear war between the two superpowers was avoided by a hair's breadth only because a naval officer on a Soviet submarine being harassed by a US destroyer refused, at the last minute, to agree to an order from his captain to fire a nuclear torpedo at an American target. When Khrushchev agreed to withdraw the missiles from Cuba as part of the deal to resolve the crisis, Che Guevara and Fidel Castro were apparently furious. Cuba had become the new bright hope of the left, and I wanted the Cuban Revolution to flourish but blowing up the world didn't seem to me the best way to achieve that.

Some of those who had left the Communist Party afterwards joined the Labour Party, perhaps encouraged by its 1960 conference decision to adopt a motion supporting unilateral nuclear disarmament. A year later, it reversed that decision. My non-joining of the Communist Party transferred to my non-joining of the Labour Party, influenced, I suspect, by what I had seen happen in the Communist Party, where adherence to the party line had compromised free thought. But I still felt more in sympathy with the *Daily Worker* than with any of the other news media and I was happy to support it in any way I could.

In March 1960, I sang with the folk group I'd joined the year before, the Galliards, at the *Daily Worker* rally in the Albert Hall. We were particularly excited to be there because Paul Robeson was the star guest. We knew, of course, about the persecution of Robeson by the witch hunters in America and admired his fearlessness in challenging the bullying interrogation by the House Un-American Activities Committee and his refusal to retract in any way his political beliefs. And, of course, we had his recordings on 78s at home when I was growing up. 'Ol' Man River' surely. 'I Dreamed I Saw Joe Hill' probably. What we didn't know, as I discovered afterwards in Martin Duberman's biography, is that he was in Moscow in 1949 when the 'anti-Zionist' (i.e., anti-Jewish) campaign was in full swing and became aware then that his great friend, Solomon Mikhoels, the director of the celebrated Moscow State Yiddish Theatre, had been brutally murdered on Stalin's orders. Another friend, the Jewish writer Itzik Feffer, was under arrest at the time but was released to meet him in his hotel room, which they both knew was bugged. A few years after that, Feffer was executed. Yet when Robeson returned to America, he denied that there was any antisemitism in Russia. 'I met Jewish people all over the place.... I heard no word about it.' Robeson's pain, anguish, shock, denial, despair were what millions of Communists must have suffered writ large. In 1961, he attempted suicide in his Moscow hotel.

Despite its being Europe's largest single-issue peace campaign, despite its direct-action wing, the Committee of 100, CND failed to change government policy on nuclear weapons. In 1964, the Labour Party, led by Harold Wilson, won power. If many in and outside the Labour Party hoped that this would signal a change of direction, they were to be disappointed. Wilson bluffed that he supported multi-lateral disarmament but could not give up Britain's nuclear deterrent. The difference between Conservative and Labour policy on this issue amounted to one Polaris submarine—four instead of the five originally commissioned.

On other issues, the Labour government was more progressive. Capital punishment was abolished, gay sex was decriminalised, abortion, within limits, was legalised, the voting age was reduced to eighteen, comprehensive schools were encouraged and grammar schools and selection discouraged, new universities and the Open University were established, working conditions were improved, and racial discrimination was outlawed (though there were stricter immigration laws). There was a serious attempt to improve Anglo-Soviet relations and Wilson refused to send military support for America's war on Vietnam. Modest achievements but, if Peter Wright's book *Spycatcher* is to be believed, they were too left-wing for the lunatic fringe of MI5, the CIA, and the millionaire press. Wilson was, in their eyes, a secret communist and a Soviet spy.

> And now my tale grows farcical—but should we laugh or
>   cry?
> For the CIA man, Angleton, names Wilson as a spy.
> And Cecil King in '68 decides to lead a coup
> Against the Wilson government, so strange it must be true.

And certain shady businessmen ask Peter for the gen
To do the dirt on Wilson, keep him out of Number Ten.
And a group of Senior Officers tell Wright of their intent
To save us from the clutches of a Labour government.
('Ballad of a Spycatcher')

The original Clause IV in the Labour Party constitution, adopted in 1918, called for 'the common ownership of the means of production, distribution and exchange' and has proved an embarrassment to the leadership ever since. Hugh Gaitskell tried to amend it and Tony Blair ditched it. In truth, the Labour Party never intended to challenge the basic structures of capitalist society, nor did it try to. With the right balance of power, the class war could be managed—this seemed to be the belief. The Attlee government nationalised (brought under state control) some basic industries and public services. It might be called public ownership but it was in no way common ownership, workers' control, or worker cooperatives. Subsequent right-wing governments had no difficulty in privatising all those state bodies, with the partial exception of the NHS.

I wasn't against a fairer, more equitable way of managing capitalism and voted for the Labour Party in 1964 and 1966. But that wasn't what I was ultimately hoping for. So what was it? There had to be a better way of organising society which didn't breed homelessness, hunger, injustice, and war. As Tony Judt would write decades later in *Ill Fares the Land*, 'Something is profoundly wrong with the way we live today.' So, I wondered, where now should I look for my alternative society? And then, lo and behold, as if in answer to my question, as the 1960s blossomed, a veritable banquet of alternative societies was being displayed for me to sample.

First up was the counterculture. Flower power. Peace and love. Free sex and psychedelic drugs. Liberate your minds. Question authority. Put flowers in your hair and in the barrels of the soldiers' guns. Live in communes and, in imitation of Native Americans, worship Mother Earth. All you need is love. Make love not war. All good slogans, but I was sceptical. I was a little too old for all that and brought up in a different tradition. And I didn't see how a peace-and-love bed-in or getting 'All You Need Is Love' to the top of the charts was going to end the war in Vietnam or help the working class shake off their chains.

> I was feeding my machine, just the usual routine
> When in marched this greasy parrot bird.
> He was gobbling down a worm, and he said he owned the firm.
> Well, who was I to doubt his word?
> He said, this firm I run has too many men by one
> And that one-too-many man is you
> I'm afraid you'll have to leave, but I love you so don't grieve
> And I said, I love you too.
> For love is the reason for life
> And life is the season of love.
> That's the way to a world without strife
> Where the eagle will fly with the dove.
> Now it was three months later, I'd devoured my last potato
> When a dagger nearly pierced my jam tart.
> Then the landlord sidled in with a chummy sort of grin
> And a rent demand tattooed on his heart.
> I was just about to pick up my oriental joss sticks
> And beat a tattoo on his face
> When this magic filled my head, all you need is love, I said
> And I wrapped him in a tender embrace.
> For love is the reason for life
> And life is the season of love,
> That's the way to a world without strife
> Where the eagle will fly with the dove.
> ('Flower Power = Bread')

There were, however, more weighty challenges to the institutions of capitalism than the hippie culture. I read Herbert Marcuse's *One-Dimensional Man* and found a resonance in his critique of the consumer society which dehumanises people, manipulates their desires so that they find their identities in the commodities capitalism pressures them to buy. Capitalism deludes its citizens into thinking they are free while at the same time repressing them. I read R. D. Laing's *The Divided Self*, which, as I understood it, asserted that mental illness might be a mechanism for escaping from a repressive reality and an impossible family situation; that insanity was a social construct, a definition imposed on the different by those who called themselves normal.

> *She was crazy, he was mad, together they danced*
> *He believed her to be the Queen of Sheba*
> *She was convinced that he was a prince*
> *And they were dancing together in the wind and the*
> * weather*
> *She was crazy, he was stark staring mad.*
> *Look here, said the man in the grey flannel skin*
> *And planted on his bald head 'Keep off the grass'*
> *It's absolutely clear that you can't dance here*
> *'Cos you haven't got a licence, your credentials won't pass*
> *And according to Subsection A in Paragraph Z*
> *You've defaulted on your payments for the upkeep of the*
> * dead.*
> ('She Was Crazy, He Was Mad')

I read Rachel Carson's *Silent Spring* which documented the damaging effect, on the environment and on human and animal life, of pesticides, which were promoted by the chemical industry in their pursuit of profit. I dipped into books by anarchist writers like Paul Goodman and Emma Goldman. I read the books by John Holt about how children learn and how children fail, an attack on an education system and a regime of testing and competition that suppresses children's natural curiosity, their desire to question and discover, and conditions them to believe that knowing the right answer is all that matters. That accorded well with my own experience.

In July 1967 I went one evening to the Roundhouse in Chalk Farm to see and hear what was going on at the Dialectics of Liberation congress. Among the radical thinkers assembled to speak during the two weeks of the congress were Laing, Marcuse, Goodman, Allen Ginsberg, and Stokely Carmichael. No women as far as I can remember, which didn't seem so shocking then as it does now. The women's liberation movement didn't get going until a few years later. I have no memory of who was on the platform the evening I went. I do remember that, when I arrived, the enormous barn-like hall was crammed full and someone was speaking or asking a question from the floor. It all seemed rather chaotic. I stood on the fringe, my preferred position, and surveyed the audience, mostly young and intense, and breathed in the heavy scent of cannabis and the atmosphere of feverish excitement. There was a feeling of urgency, as if this was the beginning of the revolution. It was unlike any political meeting I had ever been to. But if this was a revolution in the making, where was the working class?

It seemed, from what I was reading, from everything that was happening at the time, particularly in America, the civil rights movement, the Black Power movement, the demonstrations against the Vietnam War, the protests against nuclear weapons, that the organised working class was no longer seen as a force for change. Marx's prediction that the workers would rise up and overthrow the ruling class no longer applied. Workers and trade unions were now complicit in—had too much of a stake in—the system. Consumerism was overriding solidarity. This went against all that I had absorbed in my early life. Were students, oppressed minorities, the dispossessed, and the marginalised going to bring about a revolution? Well, according to Allen Ginsberg, chanting mantras or taking drugs was just as political or revolutionary an act as joining workers on the picket line. And Abbie Hoffman, cofounder of the Youth International Party (Yippies), said: 'We must abolish work and all the drudgery it represents.'

When I read about the antics of Abbie Hoffman, Jerry Rubin, and the others who founded this new political 'party,' I was amused and intrigued. More politically serious and coherent than the hippies—anarchist, socialist, antiwar, anti-money, anti–private property—its political actions were playful, imaginative, creative, and satirical. The Yippies broke all the rules. Even their name was a joke. They wanted a world where social relations were not mediated by what Marx called 'the callous cash nexus,' but, like Emma Goldman, they didn't think a revolution without dancing was a revolution worth having. They aimed to show the absurdity of a society based on competition, profit, violence, and war. They were the first, as far as I can remember, to use guerrilla theatre to catch the attention of the media. They ascended the gallery of the New York Stock Exchange and threw real and fake dollar bills to the traders below who frantically grabbed as many as they could. This spectacle was reported all around the world. I must have read about it in the *Guardian* since by then I'd given up on the *Daily Worker*, now renamed the *Morning Star*. Abbie Hoffman's promise to levitate the Pentagon and exorcise its demons was, of course, absurd, thus pointing to the absurdity of a heavily guarded government building dedicated to killing other people in war. In 1968, they nominated a pig named Pigasus as presidential candidate. This was not politics as I had known it but it was a lot more fun.

> *Won't you—come and join the party*
> *Don't you—come in uniform.*
> *Jump in—throw away your car key / khaki*

You won't have to worry
There won't be anybody to tell you what to do
If you don't want to do it—eschew it.
You can laugh—feel your heart spark an answer to your
     laughter
And you can dance—till you shake the stars apart up in the
     rafters.
We'll be—winding up the cash queues.
We'll be—tearing down the blinds.
Trumpets—blowing in the statues
All the walls are falling
There'll be time 'cos there'll be no time
And you might find your mind will grow
Why not air it—share it.
You can weave—drunken dreams and believing them is
     easy
And what you need—you can take for free and no need to
     be greedy.
Don't care—to know your name and number
Don't care— if you don't belong.
Just be—one's enough for wonder
All the cracks are healing
You can play for all the games that we play will make us
     sane
'Cos we won't be competing—just meeting.
So you can choose—and nobody will use you or refuse you
You'll never lose—'cos there'll be no rules to bruise you or
     confuse you.
('Topside Down Party')

At the Chicago Democratic Convention, the attempt by the Yippies and Students for a Democratic Society, the vanguard of what was called the New Left, to hold a free music festival as a protest against the Vietnam War was violently broken up by the riot police. We watched it on television. If the Yippies' aim was to reveal the police state behind the democratic facade, it worked. In the subsequent trial of the Chicago Seven for inciting a riot, Hoffman and Rubin ran rings round the prosecutor and the judge (also named Hoffman). They turned the trial into the absurdist farce which in reality it was. They were found guilty but their prison sentences were subsequently overturned by a court of appeal.

Yippies continued to be a presence in protests into the 1970s but the trial was effectively their last hurrah. Abbie Hoffman skipped bail when arrested on a drugs charge and lived under a false name undetected in New York, where he helped coordinate an environmental campaign to clean up the St. Lawrence River. Many in the Old Left were quick to point out that the Yippies and their allies were politically naive, unrealistic, had no class analysis, and, in believing that their actions and example could change America, did not understand how power works. True enough. But they brought into public consciousness ideas and projects that had long been part of anarchist thinking, alternative ideas and alternative ways of living and acting: food co-ops, free schools, organic farming, an underground press, concern for the environment. And, importantly, they made space for different ways of thinking about an alternative society. There was more to being human than economic activity. And there was more to life than planned economies.

The year 1968 was one of revolutions. It was also the year that Martin Luther King was assassinated and riots erupted in America's racially segregated cities. Chicago was on fire. Things were going to change. They had to. There were protest movements in Europe on both sides of the Iron Curtain. Students were at the heart of them. America's war on Vietnam was the backdrop to all of them. It was the television war, so we watched it night after night, year after year, Vietnamese children burned by napalm, their little bodies looking like 'bloody, hardened meat in a butcher's shop' in Martha Gellhorn's description. I remember singing at meetings protesting against the war and at benefits for medical aid for Vietnam but I was returning from a gig in Stourport on the day of the mass demonstration outside the American embassy in Grosvenor Square which turned violent when the protesters were assaulted by the riot police. I wasn't sorry to have missed it. That was also the year I released an LP with the poet Adrian Mitchell called *A Laugh, a Song and a Hand-Grenade*, recorded live in Bradford and Lancaster Universities. 'Whether your reaction is hostile or sympathetic, you will be stirred and disturbed,' wrote the *Daily Telegraph* reviewer. I also had a book of fifty of my songs published by Harmony Music. I see that I dedicated it to 'those who would rather not be flattened, moulded & reduced to machines, serfs, consumers, commuters, solid citizens or model soldiers.'

> One-Dimensional Man. The Divided Self.
> *The rules of the game are simple*
> *And all you have to do*
> *Is split yourself down the middle*
> *So no one can pin anything on you.*
> *Wait for the wound to harden*
> *Seal with a nerve-proof skin*
> *The rules of the game are simple*
> *And you're ready to begin.*
> *The face of the one is hidden*
> *The other one wears a mask*
> *Smiles when the cue is given*
> *Learns the right questions to ask.*
> *The brain records the answers*
> *For the parts it has to play*
> *The lips are soon word perfect*
> *And the eyes give nothing away.*
> *The face is filled with pity*

And prays for his daily bread
While the mask stands guard by the corpses
To see they don't rise from the dead.
So while one of you loves and is loving
The other one climbs alone
Sells to the highest bidder
Poisons his way to the throne.
And while one of you loves and is loving
The other one strikes it rich
And soon you'll forget to remember
Which one of you is which.
('The Rules of the Game')

The year of hope: 1968. In Europe the slogan was 'We Shall Fight, We Will Win, Paris London Rome Berlin.' It was the headline in the June '68 edition of *Black Dwarf*, the paper of the International Marxist Group, one of the growing number of radical leftist groups that were springing up in the wake of the fracturing of the Communist Party of Great Britain, which was still clinging to Moscow's coat tails. These parties, some of them Trotsky followers, shared the view that a workers' revolution was necessary but couldn't agree on how to achieve that aim. A few thrived for a time, like the International Socialists—which later became the Socialist Workers Party. Unfortunately, they all had a tendency to splinter and split and, having splintered and split once, they often found it necessary to do it again, which meant that some of these grouplets became so small as to be undetectable.

'We Shall Fight, We Will Win.' But we didn't win. In France, though, it was a close-run thing. I have a smoke-stained booklet I must have picked up when I was on holiday with the family in Paris later that year, by which time de Gaulle's party was back in government with an increased majority and the revolution had exhausted itself. It was published in June 1968 and is titled *Première histoire de la révolution de Mai.* It documents and comments on what happened every day of the revolution from 1 May until 4 June. First to protest are the students. On 1 May, Daniel Cohn-Bendit, the leader of the 'enragés' in Nanterre, is summoned before a disciplinary committee at the university. On 3 May, students in Paris demonstrating against the closure of the Sorbonne are attacked by the riot police with batons and tear gas. Around six hundred demonstrators are detained for questioning. *L'Humanité* (the Communist newspaper) attacks 'l'anarchiste allemand,' Cohn-Bendit. On 4 May, two 'enragés' are sentenced to two months' imprisonment. On 5 May, the student unions decide to strike in protest at the closure of the Sorbonne and the arrests of protesters. *L'Humanité* attacks 'Les aventuriers des groupes gauchistes, trotskystes, anarchistes' for playing into the hands of the government.

On 6 May, demonstration the whole morning in Paris. Violent clashes in the afternoon and evening. Police use tear gas grenades. Demonstrators respond with cobblestones, 422 arrests are made, around 600 students and police are injured. On 10 May: the night of the barricades. The government in a state of paralysis.

But what exactly were the students protesting about? What were they asking for? Why (as an article in my booklet asks) the students? What they were protesting against, in brief, was neocapitalism in all its aspects: its consumerism, its oppressions, its authoritarianism, its wars, its family structures, its inequalities, its injustices, and, according to the Situationists, its inauthenticity. Initially they were protesting against the hierarchical university system and its injunctions. The booklet quotes an extract from a student play where the students call for a boycott of exams. 'La grève générale! Plus d'examens. La liberté. Plus jamais d'examens.' What they wanted was to bring about a fundamentally different society. Not much to ask. To quote Cohn-Bendit: 'Nous allons vers un changement perpétuel de la société, provoqué, à chaque étape, par des actions révolutionnaires.' And students were leading the way, not because they were the most oppressed but because their social role, studying, allowed them to be the most critical of the way society conditions people. Students were situated at the hinge of two socialisation processes that were in crisis—education and the family.

The student movement proclaimed itself self-organising, independent of political parties and 'groupuscules.' It made no promises and offered no schematic instructions or easy solutions. It rejected both neo-capitalism and post-Stalin communism. The brutality of the police response to the demonstrations won sympathy for the students among the general public. When the unions declared a one-day strike in support of the students, it was the catalyst for an escalation of the revolt. The students occupied the Sorbonne. Eventually ten million workers were on strike; factories and workplaces were occupied. At one point, the government ceased to function. If I remember rightly, in the famous interview with John Lennon published in *Black Dwarf*, Tariq Ali maintained that at that point the workers should have gone on to take power. Easy to say. That would have brought the military in to defend the regime. Violence. Bloodshed. Were the French people ready for that? Revolutions achieved by violence often have unintended and unhappy consequences. In any case, violent revolution was no longer on the agenda of the Communist Party. Its trade union leaders were more interested in negotiating higher wages and better working conditions for its members. And though many workers rejected the negotiations and demanded an end to the de Gaulle government and the right to run their own factories, the moment had passed. De Gaulle dissolved the parliament and announced new elections. The dynamism and power of the uprising drained away, leaving behind regrets for what might have been and a graffiti display of creative and imaginative demands. *Il est interdit d'interdire. Je suis Marxiste-tendance Groucho. Soyez réaliste,*

demandez l'impossible. Travailleurs de tous les pays, amusez-vous.
Pouvoir à l'imagination! Sous les pavés, la plage!

In the Soviet Bloc countries, another sort of revolution was taking place which was of particular interest to those of us who retained a small hope that Soviet-style communism could still evolve into a more open and participatory society. It was called the Prague Spring. 'Socialism with a human face' suggested that previous forms of socialism lacked humanity. We watched it with interest and rising hope. Unlike in France, it was entirely peaceful and started at the top. The first secretary of the Czech Communist Party, Novotny, was replaced by Alexander Dubcek. Obviously this couldn't have happened without the approval of the Soviet Union so I didn't expect any real change in policy. But, surprisingly, I was wrong. Dubcek's Action Programme offered the freedoms available, at least nominally, in any social democratic state: freedom of speech, freedom of the media, freedom to travel abroad, an end to censorship in the arts. It also promised a decentralisation of power and an economy more geared to the production of consumer goods. For a period, the Communist Party and the people it claimed to represent seemed to be in harmony. There was an upsurge of creativity in films, books, theatre. 'Socialism cannot mean only liberation of the working people from the domination of exploiting class relations,' Dubcek wrote in the Action Programme, 'but must make more provisions for a fuller life of the personality than any bourgeois democracy.'

The invasion by the Soviet Union and other Warsaw Pact countries to crush the Prague Spring in August '68 took a hatchet to the communist movement worldwide and split it apart. Most of the European communist parties opposed it, including the CPGB, whose executive committee passed a resolution calling for the invading troops to be withdrawn. Many within the party opposed the resolution and proclaimed their support for the Soviet Union's vigilance in preventing a counterrevolution within the Communist Bloc. It was sad to see that the composer Alan Bush was one of them. He was the founder of the Workers' Music Association and had arranged folk songs for the London Youth Choir to sing. The debate raged. Journalists on the *Morning Star* took antagonistic positions. In time the opposing sides solidified into hard-line supporters of the Soviet Union, known as 'tankies,' and 'revisionists,' Euro-communists who advocated a more democratic, less sectarian form of communism more suited to Western countries, this to be achieved by constitutional means. Which side was my father on? I'm not sure but since he was still reading copies of *Soviet Weekly*, I suspect he decided it was safer to stick with what he knew.

In October 1967, Che Guevara, who we had hoped would ignite a spark of revolt that would spread like wildfire throughout Latin America, was captured and executed in Bolivia. 1968, the year of failed revolutions.

'Something is profoundly wrong with the way we live today.'

Many, having lost faith in Soviet communism, placed their hopes in other revolutions, other countries, other leaders. Some, after the Sino-Soviet split, saw China as the true future of communism and became Maoists. Apart from the Naxalites, I doubt there are many Maoists nowadays. For a time, Cuba became the beacon of hope. Then it was Chile, Nicaragua, Venezuela. We were looking for a home, somewhere over the rainbow, so, as these countries and their progressive governments struggled to survive in the face of America's plots, attacks, blockades, and CIA interventions, we gave our support to and sang for the Cuba Solidarity Campaign, the Chile Solidarity Campaign, the Nicaragua Solidarity Campaign, the Venezuela Solidarity Campaign. It wasn't so much the reality of what was happening in these countries that inspired us but what they represented: a break with monopoly capitalism, the possibility of change, a glimpse into the future. There had to be something better than this. I went on a family holiday to Cuba in 1999 and afterwards wrote a song about that experience called 'Postcards from Cuba.' Some felt it was too downbeat a picture of Cuba's 'socialist society.' But song, in my view, is a form of truth-telling. In any case, their criticism misses the point.

> Cuba's not a place, not just a poor Third World island
> It's more than just a country and it's more than its
>   achievements
> It's more than just its music and the laughter of its people
> It's an idea in the mind, it's a fragment of far-seeing
> It's a hope we keep alive in the corner of our being
> It's the spark that spreads the fire, it's the freeing of desire
> And it's sunlight out of shadow and it's dancing out of
>   sorrow
> It's the spirit of defiance, it's a vision of tomorrow.
> It's two fingers to the IMF, comeuppance for the bully
> It's a story told to children so they've something to believe in
> It's a tale we tell ourselves so we've something to believe in
> It's a brake on the machine of the New World Order
> It's refusal to submit to the rules of the marauder.
> Red and green revolution, take the power from the few.
> And it's Che in all his beauty and the dream he gave his life
>   for
> If you down enough mojitos you'll believe that dreams
>   come true.
> It's the poor demanding bread, the oppressed demanding
>   freedom
> It's the turning of the tables, it's the world turned upside
>   down.
> You can't buy everything with dollars.
> It's the voices of the voiceless bursting out into the sky
> And whatever the reality, that Cuba will not die.
> ('Postcards from Cuba')

Pouvoir à l'imagination! The power to imagine a different world, even if the means to attain it are unclear, is surely an essential first step to rejecting what is. Without a vision of an alternative way of living, there would be no alternative but to accept, as Margaret Thatcher asserted, that there is no alternative. William Morris wrote *News from Nowhere* partly in response to the utopia depicted in Edward Bellamy's novel *Looking Backward*, a form of state socialism which Morris found too narrow, authoritarian, and mechanistic. In Morris' classless society, which comes about through violent revolution, there is common ownership of the means of production; private property and money have been abolished; nature is respected and enjoyed, not exploited; and life's purpose is the pursuit of happiness.

In my mind's eye I can see him still standing
With his grey beard waving like the foam of the sea
With his shaggy hair shaking and his clear eyes shining
As he tells all who listen how different life could be.
And he rages at the wealthy with their mutilated vision
Making money the measure for everything they do
And the ugliness that kills and the lives that are broken
On the wheels that turn for the profit of the few.
And some bring the news in a sermon on the mountain
And some bring the news in a blueprint or a bulletin
But I like those who come with the passion of a vision
Like a child with a gift, like a friend with a question.
William Morris was one. In a story, in a song.
In the patterns that he wove, in the colours that he loved
In the hope that he gave, he brought the news
From nowhere ...
When our desires are freed, he said, there'll be no schools
    or prisons
No parliaments or leaders to coerce us with their laws
No property, no money to raise false divisions

And there can be an end to the endlessness of wars.
And work will be a sharing, and work will be a pleasure
When the things we make are born out of beauty and of
    need.
In a world made whole, he said, we all can be creators
Not winners and losers in a game of grab and greed.
And some bring the news ...
('Bringing the News from Nowhere')

While arguments among the various factions of the Left rumbled on through the decades, neoliberalism was advancing inexorably to occupy the institutions of Western capitalism. In 1970, the Labour government was replaced by the Tory government, which was then replaced by another Labour government, which was then ousted by the Tories led by Margaret Thatcher. In, out, in, out, let's all do the democracy dance. Eighteen years of Conservative rule followed, during which there was 'no such thing as society,' everything that could be privatised was, the miners were defeated, the trade unions were neutered, unemployment shot up, council houses were sold off, the country's manufacturing base was eroded, the numbers living in poverty soared, and inequality rose. In 1997, it was Labour's turn again.

I didn't expect much from Blair and his Third Way and support for a 'new capitalism' and the free market. I was right. Much of what the Tories did subsequently originated with New Labour: marketisation and fragmentation of the NHS, academisation of schools, the private financial initiative which contracted out public services to private companies, locking up asylum seekers in detention centres, an interventionist (i.e., criminal) foreign policy. Blair took Britain's 'special relationship' with the United States to new depths of obsequiousness well exemplified by his order to his Washington ambassador to 'get up the arse of the White House and stay there.'

The demonstration against the Iraq War on 15 February 2003 was the biggest I have ever been in, even larger than the CND marches and the demonstration against the war in Afghanistan eighteen months earlier. The Embankment was overflowing with people of all ages, waving banners, carrying placards, chanting slogans. A million of us, according to estimates, surged past the Houses of Parliament, shouting our opposition to the impending attack on Iraq and the lies used to justify it. Similar demonstrations were taking place in cities across the world. Surely they would listen. And then the political classes, in their gutlessness, their stupidity, their gullibility, their cynicism, their inhumanity, voted for war. So much for democracy.

He said: We're about to embark on a war of liberation
And when the fighting is done and the battle is won
Our tanks will roll into town and the whole population
Will gather to thank us for setting them free
And the women will throw us flowers, they will,
They'll throw us garlands of flowers—
Except for the ones whose arms have been blown off
Naturally.
We're battling one of the world's most dangerous dictators
But our bombs and rockets and shells will blow him to hell
Then we'll march into town as victorious liberators
Imagine the scene, the band is playing
The children are running to greet us, yes,
The happy children are running—
Except for the ones whose legs have been blown off
That goes without saying.
Now let's be clear, we haven't come here as invaders
In this benighted neck of the woods, we're a force for good
Just think of yourselves as modern-day crusaders
And Iraqi people forevermore
Will remember us in their prayers, they will,

They'll remember us in their prayers—
Except for the ones whose heads have been blown off
That's for sure.
('General Lockjaw Briefs the Troops')

For many, the war on Iraq was the last straw. Labour Party support and membership drained away. In 2007, the leader changed his name to Gordon Brown, just in time to bail out the bankers after the financial crash.

Robespierre is wagging his finger
Karl Marx is scratching his head
They ought to be shooting the bankers
But they're giving them money instead.
The plebs should be storming the ramparts
And whetting the guillotine's blade
Singing capitalism's in crisis
So where are the barricades?
('Where Are the Barricades?')

And in 2010 Labour lost the election. By this time, I was convinced that Western democracy was a farce, offering two slightly different versions of much the same.

It's like an endless game of cricket
Each team takes turns at the wicket
While we watch and cheer and boo
And that, I fear, is all we do.
One team's in, the other's out
Then it's turn and turn about
This lot's out, that lot comes in
Different faces, same old spin
Same old system, same old lies
Same old drive to privatise.
Democracy, a funny game
You put a cross against a name

The Chartists and the Suffragettes
Fought for this privilege, don't forget
So do your duty, make your choice
Thank them for giving you a voice.
Next thing they've taken your consent
To form a bleeding government.
Democracy, it's called democracy
Aren't you happy that you live in a democracy?
That cross you innocently appended
Has consequences unintended.
Remember 1997?
For one brief spring a glimpse of heaven.
We thought, we hoped, at least, to see
A fairer-run society.
But in the end what did we get?
A hollow system run on debt
A system where the market rules
Where wealth buys peerages and schools
Where everything is done to groom us
To behave like good consumers
A culture of celebrity—
Oh look, we're on CCTV.
Dodgy arms deals? Well, why not?
Asylum seekers? Let them rot.
Lock them up for their own good
Campsfield, Harmondsworth, Yarls Wood.
Tough on crime and immigration
Anti-terrorist legislation
Used to criminalise dissent
None of that is what I meant.
Tuition fees, ASBOs galore
The penalty for being poor
And worst of all, war after war
That isn't what I voted for.

Democracy. It's called democracy.
Aren't you happy that you live in a democracy?
Remember Blair's peroration?
Education, education, education.
Children tested, children stressed
Endless targets, SATs obsessed.
City gamblers? Must reward them.
Post offices? Can't afford them.
Hail the City's reckless greed
Bonuses are guaranteed
To soar into the stratosphere.
The rich grow richer every year.
Hedge fund speculators? Loaded.
Civil liberties? Eroded.
Torture? MI5 complicit.
Not a pretty picture, is it?
The system's riding on a bubble.
Now the whole shebang's in trouble.
It must end—it does—in tears
After thirteen wasted years
Ends in one almighty crash
So give the bankers bags of cash.
Their greed it was that helped to rob
A million workers of their jobs
But still the system, so it goes,
Must be maintained—as wider grows
The gap between the rich and poor
And still they're wasting lives on war.
That isn't what I voted for.
Democracy. It's called democracy.
Aren't you happy that you live in a democracy?
Democracy, so fine, so fair
How come it landed us with Blair?
Gave us as our leader one

Who thinks that he is God's own son.
A tricky politician who
Believes what he believes is true.
Some think him bumptious, vain, and smug
Regard him as a well-bred thug.
But Blair's an amiable guy.
Look, he wouldn't harm a fly.
But when he smiles, children die.
I met murder on the stair
He had a mask like Tony Blair
He cracked a smile, he cracked a joke
A pretty straightforward sort of bloke
And a crusading politician
Democracy, that's his mission
To spread it here, to spread it there
So everyone can have a share.
Western democracy, the prize
The surest way to civilise
The backward nations, set them free
And if they dare to disagree
They must be bombed for their objections
Until they learn to hold elections.
They call this, I forgot to mention, Humanitarian
*   intervention.*
And did the slaughter his war brought
Ever give him pause for thought?
And did the chaos he created
A country smashed and devastated
The tortured, the incarcerated
The shattered millions who fled
The maimed, the half a million dead
Cause him to doubt or hesitate?
Or did he simply calculate
That this was a price that was worth paying

And salved his conscience by praying?
Well, afterwards, you couldn't get
From Blair a smidgeon of regret.
Indeed this unrepentant man
Declared a wish to bomb Iran.
This liar, fantasist, and faker
Will answer only to his maker.
Now think on this—for all his crimes
We elected Blair three times.
Democracy. It's called democracy.
Aren't you happy that you live in a democracy?
Ah democracy. God bless democracy.
Now it's time to sing the praises of democracy.
('Talking Democracy Blues')

In 1986 I was invited to sing at a political song festival in East Berlin, organised by the Free German Youth, the official youth movement of the German Democratic Republic. What sort of political song, I wondered, would be acceptable in an authoritarian regime like the GDR? Eight years earlier, I'd sung at a concert in West Berlin in support of Rudolf Bahro, who was in prison in East Germany for writing and allowing to be published in West Germany his book *The Alternative*, a critique of 'actually existing socialism.' I'm not sure how I got that gig. I seem to remember that Tariq Ali had something to do with arranging it. I do remember the vastness of the hall, the noisy excitement emanating from the audience, and the chaotic way it ended. Wolf Biermann, probably Germany's best-known singer-songwriter, was closing the concert but his allotted time was cut short because the concert was over-running. Some in the audience shouted for him to carry on singing after the concert was due to end, but another group ran onto the stage and objected that it would mean paying extra and they were against star performers indulging their egos. All this was explained by my interpreter. Biermann had, of course, been banned from singing in East Germany and then exiled from the country.

What sort of political song festival bans its best-known songwriter from participating? It was February, very cold, snow on the streets. I had learned a little German from a BBC Kontakte Audio course. In the event, I was allotted an official student interpreter and anyway most of the Germans I met could converse in English. One of the unlikely phrases in the course I'd been asked to learn was *Wo sind die Elefanten?* (Where are the elephants?) I never actually asked any Germans that question, though I was tempted, but decided to tuck it into my memory box in case it came in useful later. As I expected, the festival's definition of political song was any song that drew attention to the failings of Western capitalism. The failings of Soviet-style socialism were not on the agenda. The audience responded to 'Don't Get Married, Girls' with bemusement. The personal was not yet political in the GDR. And anyway, they didn't have that problem (whatever it was) there. There was a curious moment at the end of Pete Seeger's concert when he sang 'We Shall Overcome' and everyone stood up in solidarity. But solidarity with whom? Who, in the context of an authoritarian state that shoots or imprisons its citizens if they attempt to escape, is 'we'?

While I was at the festival, I started writing a song which I decided I would call 'Wo Sind die Elefanten?' It didn't go anywhere. I needed to know the end of the story. Three years later demonstrations calling for 'socialism with a human face' and greater freedoms shook the East German government. When Gorbachev stated that he would not countenance military intervention, the fate of the regime was sealed. The demonstrations grew, the government's concessions and reforms were too little and too late, and on 9 November 1989 the Wall fell and thousands poured across the border. I remember sitting in my living room in my house in Wembley, watching it on TV with mixed feelings. On the one hand, I believed that a regime sustained by repression did not deserve to survive. On the other, I wasn't happy about this dramatic victory for West German capitalism. But there was no stopping it now. In Poland, Czechoslovakia, Hungary, Bulgaria, and even Romania, popular pressure pushed aside Communist governments, largely peacefully. And then the Soviet Union itself began to disintegrate, its constituent republics peeling away until, at the end of 1991, Gorbachev resigned, Yeltsin replaced him, and the Communist Party was dissolved. The seventy-four-year experiment was over.

I no longer invested any of my hopes in the Soviet Bloc countries but others, like my father, were disorientated by what was happening and could not come to terms with it. And I still hadn't written my song. I couldn't yet see how to approach a song about such world-shattering events. What story should I tell?

One thing I was sure of. New songs would be written in response to these ongoing dramatic upheavals. Political song was surely due for a revival. No surprise then that I and a group of like-minded singers, songwriters, musicians—Robb Johnson, Sandra Kerr, Jim Woodland, Janet Russell, Frankie Armstrong, Roy Bailey—founded the Political Song Network and launched the Red and Green Umbrella Club, a monthly venue for new songs. It attracted enthusiastic audiences.

And the debate raged. What did the collapse of actually existing socialism mean for our politics and our songwriting? It was an exciting time. A division was opening up between those of us, including the Red and Green Umbrella Club founders, who embraced a broader definition of 'political' that encompassed green issues and sexual and personal politics and those who followed the Communist Party line that the class war was all-important and political song should focus on the lives and struggles of the working class. The arguments were not always comradely, unsurprisingly since those who had pinned their hopes on the Soviet Union felt betrayed. In one issue of the Political Song Network maga-zine, the writer Mike Rosen described Stalinism as a tyranny as bad as any in human history and attacked the folk song movement, or more particularly the political and protest part of it, for being bound up with 'the revolting antics of stalinist and maoist parties.' In the same issue was a song by Karl Dallas. Called 'Djugashvili,' it sang the praises of the great leader Joseph Stalin. I remember coming under attack at an event called The Red Megaphone, a commemoration of the life and work of Ewan MacColl who had died in October 1989, because in a talk on songwriting I had ventured to suggest that MacColl's workerist approach to songwriting was no longer fruitful. I didn't mind being attacked for my argu-ments but I was upset when the historian Ralph Samuel, who had been a Communist Party member, told the audience that my views invalidated my songs.

'The end of history,' wrote Francis Fukuyama. I knew that was nonsense. Yes, it looked as if the planned economy and public ownership of the means of production had lost out to market capitalism, but the struggle for a better world would surely continue.

A few years later, the group who had founded the Red and Green Umbrella Club, plus Reem Kelani, Grace Petrie, Peggy Seeger, and Boff Whalley, formed the Anti-Capitalist Roadshow. In the tradition of the Almanac Singers, we gave concerts in towns and cities all over the country, using song to challenge the Thatcherite agenda. Our ultimate aim, of course, was to spark an uprising that would overthrow capitalism and usher in that kind, just, peaceful society we had long dreamed of. Alas, the power of song has its limits. Nevertheless, my collaboration with those friends and colleagues was one of the few hopeful, enjoyable experiences of that bleak decade.

For the many thousands of Communists who had kept the faith, the seemingly endless era of Thatcherism must have been doubly bleak. I felt sad for them. A lifetime of struggle for a cause that had betrayed them. My father had died in January 1989 before the collapse of his hopes, his dreams, everything he believed in. He would anyway not have wanted to see it. He was mentally alert to the end so he was certainly aware of the changes that were taking place in the communist world. As I remember, he did not entirely approve of Gorbachev's reforms. By the end of his life, I think he'd given up on the human race. A short time before he died, he had collapsed in the garden of his flat in Wembley and lost consciousness. Other flat dwellers found him and revived him. He said he wished they hadn't. It was, he said, a beautiful experience, dying, so peaceful.

One issue of the *Red and Green Song Magazine* was devoted to songs about the fall of the Berlin Wall. It included, if I remember correctly, Charlie King's 'The Wall,' Robb Johnson's 'Winter Turns to Spring,' and this song that I finally managed to write, 'Wo Sind die Elefanten?':

> *East Berlin in February, 20 degrees below*
> *Hurrying figures hunched against the darkness and the*
>   *snow*
> *And I watch them file down Karl Marx Allee, queuing at*
>   *the lights*
> *So they can cross the road and fade into the night.*
> *If I could only find the German I once learned from the*
>   *BBC*
> *I could ask them: Are they happy? Are they free?*
> *But only one phrase lingers on from Lesson Three.*
> *It remains in my brain, like a lonely refrain*
> *Like a song that has no ending and it's sending me insane*
> *And I say—*
> Wo sind die Elefanten? *Faces turn and stare.*
> *The question sparks no answer as it dies upon the air.*
> Wo sind die Elefanten? *No one wants to know*

Or dares disturb the silence of the snow
And I thought I knew the answer long ago.
The young man wears a party badge, a clenched fist in his
    head
And his speech marks out the future, and for him the
    future's red
And I watch him as he builds a wall to keep the shadows
    out
From an ordered world that has no room for doubt.
Does he believe the chants he marches to, the slogans and
    the lies?
Or does he calculate that that's the way to rise?
And is that certainty he wears or a disguise?
And again in my brain there's this lonely refrain
Like a song that has no ending and it's sending me insane
And I say—
Wo sind die Elefanten? What's the latest news?
Are they doing tricks in circuses or locked in concrete zoos?
Wo sind die Elefanten? He doesn't seem to know
Or won't disturb the silence of the snow.
And I thought I knew the answer long ago.
Now the Berlin Wall has crumbled like sandcastles in the
    sea
And there's been a revolution where it wasn't meant to be
And I've watched the crowds on TV as if waking in the
    dawn
They see the old world dead, the new world not yet born.
And are they bright with hopes of videos and dishwashing
    machines
Big Macs, cosmetics, porno magazines
And Dallas on their television screens?
And I hear everywhere cash is king, grab your share—
In the corridors of choices, are there voices still that dare
To ask it—?

Wo sind die Elefanten? Nomads roaming free.
Once they ruled the continents from the mountains to the
sea.
Wo sind die Elefanten? No one seems to know
Or cares to break the silence of the snow.
And I thought I knew the answer long ago.
Once elephants roamed Hampstead Heath, and still in my
mind's eye
I see them silhouetted against the eastern sky
With their trunks raised up in triumph to salute the rising
sun—
And then one day I woke, and they were gone.
Those strange fantastic creatures with their gentle, caring
ways
Too large to fit the landscape of these days
Where nothing is preserved unless it pays.
But the poor are still poor, and there's greed, and there's
war
And the markets junk out squalor that the dollar cannot
cure
So tell me—
Wo sind die Elefanten? Weeping for their dead.
Circulating sadly round the dried-up riverbed.
Wo sind die Elefanten? Vanished with the snow.
Were they just a dream of long ago?
A story for a child I used to know?

It is 22 June 2020. My eighty-sixth birthday. Exactly
seventy-nine years since the milkman brought us that fateful
news. It's been a long road. And it hasn't led to the hoped-for
promised land somewhere over the rainbow.

Now we're in the middle of a pandemic. Apart from a
local walk from time to time, I've been stuck at home for
three months, and this vicarious life is beginning to pall.
We have a government, elected with a large majority last

December (it's called democracy), whose every word is a lie and whose incompetence has given us the third-highest number of coronavirus deaths in the world. So where is my alternative society? When Jeremy Corbyn was unexpectedly elected Labour Party leader in 2015, there was hope for real change and thousands joined or rejoined the Labour Party. Its manifesto for the 2019 election promised a Green New Deal, creating a million new jobs and drastically cutting carbon emissions by 2030, an end to austerity and the gig economy, bringing the railways, energy, and water systems into democratic public ownership, increased investment in public transport and social housing, a cap on rents, an end to homelessness, greater environmental protection and a new Clean Air Act to reduce air pollution, an end to NHS privatisation, a higher living wage, greater workers' rights and a shorter working week, an end to the hostile environment of the immigration system, recognising the state of Palestine, and more. The renewal of the Trident nuclear weapons system would, however, go ahead, though Corbyn himself has been a consistent supporter of CND. Apart from that, it was the most radical manifesto of my lifetime.

Whether those that control the levers of power in the country would have allowed these plans to be put into practice is a moot point. In the event, Corbyn and the Corbyn project were systematically undermined by the media, including the so-called liberal *Guardian* and the BBC, the fake antisemitism campaign invented by the Zionist bodies and the Israel lobby, the Blairite Labour MPs, the divisions over Brexit, and Corbyn's own naiveté. The election was a disaster. The Labour Party is now back in the hands of the Right and 'moderates' and is continuing a witch hunt of Corbyn supporters, anti-Zionist Jews, and critics of Israel. I expect no real change from this Labour Party or from parliamentary politicking. Opposition when it comes will come from the street. So the worldwide Black Lives Matter demonstrations resulting from the murder of George Floyd are a gleam of hope. When the statue of the slave trader Edward Colston was toppled in Bristol and dumped into the harbour, the government, whose austerity policies have been responsible for the deaths of thousands and the impoverishment of millions, condemned it as 'criminal damage.' The new Labour Party leader, Keir Starmer, said it was 'completely wrong.'

How will this pandemic and the economic catastrophe it has caused pan out? 'Because things are the way they are, things will not stay the way they are,' Brecht wrote. That seems certain. But there's no guarantee that they won't change for the worse. The Conservative Party, led by an unprincipled liar and chancer, is determined to exit the EU with no deal so that they can make a trade deal with the United States. This will mean junking the environmental protection and animal welfare and food standards that in their election manifesto they pledged to uphold. And they will use the excuse of the economic collapse to reinstate austerity and allow the free market free rein. The prospect is dire. Who will stop them?

The pandemic, writes Arundhati Roy, 'offers us a chance to rethink the doomsday machine we have built for ourselves. Nothing could be worse than a return to normality.... It is a portal, a gateway between one world and the next.' Yes. But what will this new world look like? And how will it come about? Capitalism will eat itself, we used to say. But will it, in the process, eat everything else, including the future of the planet and all that live in it? If capitalism continues to ravage the earth and its resources in its drive for profit, there will be no future.

'Communism promised'— but it didn't deliver. All I know is that the end of Soviet-style communism was not the end of history, that there is always hope, that people will always struggle against what is and will always envision a better, kinder, saner, more peaceful, and harmonious way of living together and respecting the natural world and those who make their home in it.

> *You poor take courage, you rich take care*
> *This earth was made a common treasury for everyone to*
>   *share*
> *All things in common, all people one*
> *We come in peace …*
> ('The World Turned Upside Down')

2

The Power of Song

Some decades ago, I went to see a Sunday morning Socialist Film Co-op showing of a film about the Wobblies at the Renoir in London. In the discussion afterwards, Tony Benn voiced this criticism: the problem with the Wobblies, he said, was that they failed to form a political party, unlike in Britain where the unions gave birth to the Labour Party. To which I was tempted to reply that the problem with the Labour Party is that it doesn't have any songs, apart, of course, from 'The Red Flag' which it insists on singing to the wrong tune.

The Wobblies, the Industrial Workers of the World, were anarcho-syndicalists, believers in the one big union and the one big strike that would break the power of the bosses forever. For twenty years at the beginning of the twentieth century, they were a singing crusade on behalf of the poorest, most exploited workers in America: loggers, railroad mechanics, copper miners, hop pickers, textile workers, the unskilled working stiffs despised by the craft unions of the American Federation of Labor, immigrants many of them, ill-educated and ill-organised. Songs transformed them, elevated them, organised them, united them, enthused them with hope and courage. They took popular songs and 'Starvation Army' hymns and turned the words inside out, sharpening them with a subversive irony. They rolled the language, humour, and experience of life at the bottom into something exuberant and immensely singable—not poetry, perhaps, but to the point.

> *Praise boss when morning work bells chime*
> *Praise him for bits of overtime*
> *Praise him whose wars we love to fight*
> *Praise him fat leech and parasite.*

With no mass media, no technology, no money, and nothing but their own voices, their own energy and imagination, and *The Little Red Song Book* to fan the flames of discontent, they spread the songs from Spokane, where they triumphed in the fight for free speech, down to the copper mines of Bisbee, Arizona, and across to Lawrence, Massachusetts, where they won the famous Bread and Roses Strike of textile workers in 1912. They sang in meeting halls and soup kitchens; they sang on freight trains and at the funeral of Joe Hill in Chicago; they sang in street demonstrations and in prison cells. 'Sing!' Mother Jones told the women in Greensburg, Pennsylvania, when they'd been put in prison for demonstrating during a miners' strike. 'Sing the whole night long and don't stop for anyone.... Just you all sing and sing.' And so they did, driving the sheriff to distraction until he released them.

The power of song. For those at the bottom, for those with nothing much else but their own voices (and, it would appear, nothing much to sing about), song has always been important. Because song, as any football fan knows, has the power to make us feel less alone, to unite us, to create a sense of solidarity. Think of songs like 'We Shall Overcome,' 'Which Side Are You On?,' 'Solidarity Forever,' 'El Pueblo Unido Jamás Será Vencido,' 'H Bomb's Thunder,' 'You'll Never Walk Alone,' 'Land of Hope and Glory' or the Ulster battle hymn, 'Oh God Our Help in Ages Past.' (I include the last two to point out that the Left doesn't have a monopoly on this sort of song.) Surely the Diggers on St. George's Hill sang to keep up their spirits as they faced attack from the soldiers.

Your houses they pull down, stand up now, stand up now,
Your houses they pull down, stand up now.
Your houses they pull down to fright poor men in town
But the gentry must come down and the poor shall wear
    the crown
Stand up now, Diggers all.

And listening to the fiercely joyous song of the French Revolution, 'La Carmagnole,' it's not difficult to understand how it would have strengthened the resolve of the *sans culottes* to bring down the monarchy and the aristocracy.

Dansons la Carmagnole
Vive le son, vive le son
Dansons la Carmagnole
Vive le son
Du canon.

All revolutions and social movements have their songs—the Chartists, the Suffragettes, antinuclear protesters, Greenham Common women, anti-apartheid demonstrators, civil rights activists. The best and most liberating bubble up from below. Those movements where singing and song-making are a spontaneous activity (as opposed to movements where singing is part of a disciplined ritual imposed from above) tend to be nonauthoritarian and nonhierarchical, as the Wobblies were. They have, like the Wobblies, a clear-cut, simplified view of the world and of who the enemy is. And they have a shared vision. For the IWW, the strike was never an end in itself but a means to the transformation of society into a workers' commonwealth. This vision of a new world, which merges with the hobo's dream of the Big Rock Candy Mountain, lies at the heart of their songwriting.

Which raises the question of why in the labour movement in England (I mean England, not Scotland or Ireland) there is no body of song equivalent to that produced by the

Wobblies. There is no tradition of politically conscious, singable songs like those generated by the Appalachia coal-mining communities in the 1930s as they battled to become unionised: songs like Aunt Molly Jackson's 'I Am a Union Woman,' Sarah Ogun Gunning's 'I Hate the Capitalist System,' Jim Garland's 'I Don't Want Your Millions, Mister,' and Florence Reece's 'Which Side Are You On?' There are industrial folk songs, songs about hard times and poverty, pit disasters and evictions, strikes and lockouts. They linger on in areas where the tradition is strongest, as in northeast England, or in pockets of the folk revival, but they never entered the mainstream of the labour movement. Perhaps because they lacked a consciously political perspective or because they were thought to be lacking in high seriousness, they never found favour with the decision-makers in labour organisations.

At about the same time as Jim Connell was composing 'The Red Flag,' Tommy Armstrong, the famous pit poet of Durham County, was writing a very different sort of song about the Durham lockout of 1892. Raising the scarlet standard high was not uppermost in Armstrong's mind. More to the point, as far as he was concerned, was the threat to the masters of a severe lashing and boils on the backside if they didn't mend their ways.

The politically conscious songs tended to be written by literary gents. *Songs for Socialists*, published by the Fabian Society in 1912, contains a number of these labour anthems. (Jim Connell was certainly not a literary gent but his song belongs in that mould.) 'Ye sturdy sons of labour,' they exhort. 'Awake! Arise! Bear the flag unfurled and the banner aloft!' March forward side by side to battle like a mighty river for Liberty, Brotherhood, Justice, the Cause. Even the best of them, by William Morris, Edward Carpenter, and Ernest Jones, though technically competent, are stodgy, humourless, and virtually unsingable. The working classes may have dutifully sung them when the formal occasion demanded, but they never really took to them, preferring something more earthy and less worthy. So the anthems were left to gather dust and moulder, apart from 'The Red Flag' that lives on, embarrassing generations of Labour Party activists and MPs who can't quite get their tongues round it. And reverting to Jim Connell's original sprightly Irish tune, 'The White Cockade' (banned, I imagine, by some bureaucrat from the Social Democratic Federation for being too lightweight), does not, despite Billy Bragg's efforts, get round the problem of its archaisms and literary pretensions.

So now there is a silence at the heart of the labour movement. Of course, historically there have been strike songs. The women's songbook *My Song Is My Own* has collected some of them, like the 'Idris Strike Song' of 1911 and the 'Song for the Trico Women Workers,' sung to the tune of 'John Brown's Body' on the picket line during the successful equal pay strike of 1976.

> *The management are not prepared to give us what we ask*
> *They're saying that they can't believe we're equal to the task*
> *But if men can do what we do then their argument's a*
>   *farce*
> *So we want equal pay.*
> *Equal pay for women workers*
> *Equal pay for women workers*
> *Equal pay for women workers*
> *We want equal pay.*

But there isn't a pool of singable shared songs to draw on when spirits need refreshing on demonstrations, picket lines, in political meetings, and on the barricades. Nowadays on demonstrations there are chants and slogans but little if any singing, despite the efforts of the political choirs.

Wouldn't it enliven a Labour Party branch meeting if the first item on the agenda was a twenty-minute singsong? Somehow, I doubt it ever happens. When I joined the mass pickets outside Grunwick during the strike of 1977, I didn't hear one song, not even 'The Red Flag,' except, on one occasion, the trade union leader Norman Willis entertained us with a rendering of 'The Man That Waters the Workers' Beer.' Nobody joined in. On one mass picket, I dusted off my banjo and went with Hackney Music Workshop to encourage the assembled thousands to sing (mostly the standard American solidarity songs). There was polite attention and applause. But no singing. Perhaps, now that Jeremy Corbyn has activated the grassroots, new songs will spring up and become common currency. Ohhh, Jeremy Corbyn!

The power of song. In Soweto, women and children sang as they were shot down by the police. The Viet Cong carried song sheets into battle with them. Civil rights demonstrators in the States sang as they were being attacked by Alsatian dogs, fire hoses, and billy clubs because it made them feel less alone, less afraid. The importance of the New Song movement in Chile can be gauged by the lengths the junta went to to destroy it. Colonising powers have always attempted to root out indigenous music and culture. A defeated people does not sing. Perhaps the converse is also true—a movement that has no songs is already defeated.

3

Stand Up, Stand Up for Song

People often describe songs they particularly like as poetry. It's meant to be a compliment. To laud a songwriter as a poet is supposed to be the ultimate accolade. From my perspective, it's more like the kiss of death. It downgrades song. The inference is that the song lyric is not important enough or creative enough in itself but must be raised in status by labelling it poetry. It misunderstands the different ways in which song and poetry work.

In England, though not, for instance, in France, most people have low expectations of song. Simon Armitage, a poet, was quoted in the *Guardian* as saying that 'good lyrics often do what you are taught not to do in poems: clichés, cheesy rhymes, mixed metaphors.' This, the condescending voice of poetry, is an insult to those of us who take the song form seriously and suggests Armitage has been feeding his brain on an exclusive diet of crap songs in the marketplace. Song is not an inferior form of poetry. It's a creative form in its own right and should be judged by the same high standards as any other art form. A good song is as difficult to write as a good poem. The technical restraints are, in fact, greater. But a song is not a poem.

Bob Dylan was awarded the Nobel Prize in Literature not for being a sparky songwriter but 'for having created new poetic expressions within the great American song tradition,' whatever that means. In my view, he should have refused it. Why allow his free-roaming songs to be tamed and safely tucked up in bed inside a box marked 'literature'? As for 'new poetic expressions,' some might argue that the nearer his songs got to 'poetry' the worse his songwriting became. From fine songs like 'A Hard Rain's Gonna Fall' and 'The Lonesome Death of Hattie Carroll,' rooted in an observable reality, to the free-floating images of 'Gates of Eden' seems less like an ascent into poetry than a descent into gibberish.

One of the problems with songwriters who aspire to poetry is the belief that poetry equals mystification and obfuscation and that poetic language should be clotted and opaque. This is a delusion.

> *And I always thought: the very simplest words*
> *Must be enough. When I say what things are like*
> *Everyone's heart must be torn to shreds.*
> *That you'll go down if you don't stand up for yourself*
> *Surely you see that.*
> —Bertolt Brecht

In his memoir, *The Mayor of MacDougal Street*, Dave Van Ronk, who was, I guess, Dylan's political mentor and who never downplays Dylan's talent, made some shrewd observations about the way songwriting in the sixties became self-consciously poetic, absorbing influences from, for instance, French symbolist poets. The more self-consciously artistic the songs became, he writes, the less interest he had in it:

> The whole artistic mystique is one of the great traps of this business, because down that road lies unintelligibility. Dylan has a lot to answer for there because after a while he discovered that he could get away with anything—he was Bob Dylan and people would take whatever he wrote on faith. So he could do something

like 'All Along the Watchtower,' which is simply a mistake from the title on down: a watchtower is not a road or a wall, and you can't go along it.

He is surely right. Or maybe he isn't. Who knows? Who knows what goes on inside the mind of Bob Dylan? The answer, my friend, is blowing in some windy corner of the brain of professor Christopher Ricks, who has spent half a lifetime obsessively analysing and deciphering everything Dylan has ever doodled and unearthing, or inventing, meanings that even Bob himself was unaware of. True, he recognises that song is not poetry and doesn't exist without the music but that doesn't stop him from scrutinising Dylan's texts in order to prove—what? That Dylan is more than a songwriter, he's a poet. Because being just a songwriter, even a talented songwriter, even a brilliant songwriter is not good enough.

Song and poetry are in many ways opposites. Poetry is subjective. The poet observes closely and interprets for us. The 'I' in a poem is nearly always the poet. The 'I' in a song should not be the songwriter but a persona, an adopted character. A proper use of rhyme is, in my view, important in song. Not so, of course, in poetry. Song at its best tells stories about people—like theatre, where the playwright does not intrude into the drama. And, like theatre, song only exists in performance. Making things up is what song is about. Of course, this is not true, on the whole, of song in the market-place which purports to tell us what the singer/songwriter is feeling and asks for our sympathy. And our money. This is the song lyric as a not very interesting commodity. It is not true either of many political/protest songs which usually tell us what to think and which are important in creating solidarity, particularly on the barricades (where are the barricades?), but which are not the best use of the song form. Song should be a work of the imagination. The only thing song and poetry share is a love and careful use of words. Show me a song-writer who strains to deliver 'the poetical' and I will show you—Leonard Cohen.

Dylan came to songwriting via the Great Folk Scare of the 1960s. He listened to and absorbed everything he heard from Woody Guthrie and Ramblin' Jack Elliott to Martin Carthy and so knew, even when he thought he was Rimbaud reincarnated, that song is best as a narrative form. Cohen came from the world of poetry, and this partially accounts for the weaknesses in his songwriting. For example, the range of his subject matter is remarkably small. In fact, his interests as expressed in his songs can be narrowed down to one: himself.

Moreover, he had no imagination. He was incapable of making up stories, of inventing characters, which are the warp and weft of song. As he himself said, 'I have a very poor imagination, so I'm a kind of journalist reporting as accurately as I can.' That means he is mostly reduced to, as he says, being a kind of journalist reporting on his various relationships, the most uncreative use of the song form.

And I have other criticisms. His song forms are limited, his technique slipshod. In 'So Long, Marianne,' for instance, he has perfect rhymes (park/dark), half-rhymes (palm/home), and non-rhymes (much/us). Does it matter? That's like asking if it matters that the table you've just made has one leg shorter than the others. 'A good lyric should not only have something to say but also a way of saying it as clearly and forcefully as possible—and that involves rhyming cleanly' (Stephen Sondheim). Or, at least being consistent.

It's not, of course, that Cohen didn't understand rhyme. 'Suzanne,' the song that catapulted him from poetry into songwriting, was written as a poem, and, though I distrust its obscure (because private) references, its pretentious Jesus verse, its flow of words and images that bypass the brain, it is more carefully written than much of what he wrote as song.

This suggests to me that, like Simon Armitage, he considered song as an inferior form of poetry so it didn't matter, and he could get away with 'cheesy rhymes,' padded out lines ('Your letters they all say'), nonsensical similes ('Your hair upon the pillow / Like a sleepy golden storm'), metaphors strained and verging on the risible ('I'm standing on a ledge and your fine spider web / Is fastening my ankle to a stone').

When he ventures away from *me me me* songs, he becomes vague and obfuscatory, throwing in religious references and hinting at a profundity he cannot attain. What I hear when I listen to 'Hallelujah' or 'First We Take Manhattan' is a hollow drum roll signifying nothing.

Song is a way of engaging with the world. Cohen's songs do not do that; or, on the rare occasions when they do, as in his reworking of the story of Isaac, which was done rather better by Wilfred Owen, he becomes curiously evasive and ambiguous. It is difficult to know, from his songs, whether he had any view on what was happening in the public world, as opposed to what was happening in his personal relationships. He enlisted in the Israeli army in the Yom Kippur War of 1973. In 2009, he gave a concert in Tel Aviv, thus breaking the boycott called for by Palestinian civil society. Presumably, he was a supporter of the Jewish state, but his commitment didn't emerge into song.

Dylan too went through a Zionist phase, becoming a supporter of the extremist, racist rabbi Meir Kahane. And his support of Israel was filtered into a song (that it is an embarrassingly bad song is not the point here) called 'The Neighborhood Bully.' Because if you're a songwriter and you feel strongly about something, that's what you do. But perhaps Cohen was afraid that political commitment would not sit well with his image as a romantic poet.

4

Me, Georges Brassens, and the Last Chance

A Shaggy Dog Story

My first solo recording was in 1962, an EP for Topic Records called *Songs for City Squares*. It wasn't my choice of title. I followed that up with an LP called *Songs for Sceptical Circles*. What next? *Songs for Truculent Triangles*? *Songs for Quirky Quadrangles*?

A reviewer of my EP, in *Audio and Record Review*, suggested I might 'ripen into a British Brassens.' I wasn't altogether happy about the 'ripen,' as if I was some sort of green fruit, but I presumed it was intended as a compliment. I knew nothing about Georges Brassens at the time. The name, however, did ring a distant bell.

Wind back four years and I am in Israel with my nylon-string Kessler guitar and my five-string banjo earning my bread by singing with two young American women in a group called Ha Nodedim. We often used to sing in The Last Chance, a kind of homemade nightclub in Beersheva. The man who booked us, Leon Hellman, was the son of a New York rabbi. His passions were collecting spiritual stones and Mahalia Jackson. I don't think he was particularly enamoured of our singing, but he calculated, with some justification, that Beersheva's male population would flock to The Last Chance to ogle these two very attractive American women. (Don't go away. We will find our way back to Brassens in good time.)

By the way, in 1983 I wrote a songspiel about The Last Chance called, unsurprisingly, *The Last Chance*.

There had been a sandstorm the first time we performed there. It had hit Beersheva at the dawn of a grey gritty morning, swirled through the streets, blinded the window panes, choked the inhabitants, and swept on into the Negev. The Last Chance was in a chaotic state. The walls loomed with strange excrescences. The windows peered at you through surrealist designs. On one strip of wall was written 'L'homme n'est pas fait pour le travail. La preuve c'est que ça le fatigue.' A wheel, hung with wire and tin cans, deformed wood, and lacquered stones, balanced oddly on a twisted tree trunk. A branch of wood bowed, saint-like, over the pillared entrance. A signpost stating that Ramle was 45 kilometres away directed the customer towards the bar.

Ramle. I remember something about Ramle. Ramle and Lydda. It was from there that, in July 1948, seventy thousand Palestinians were driven out on the orders of Ben Gurion. It was known as the Death March. Hundreds died. One who survived by drinking his own urine was a young medical student named George Habash. Afterwards he founded the Popular Front for the Liberation of Palestine, the organisation that committed a number of terrorist acts and in 2002 assassinated Rehavam Ze'evi, Israel's racist minister of tourism. So it goes. (This is, of course, by the way, but life, after all, is not lived in straight lines.)

Mahalia Jackson was on the turntable singing her heart out. I thought of Mahalia recently as I watched Houston and half of Asia sinking under the waves.

> *Didn't it rain, children*
> *Talk 'bout rain, oh my Lord*
> *Didn't it, didn't it, didn't it, oh my Lord*
> *Didn't it rain?*

Listening to Mahalia's Jesus songs and searching the wadi for artistically shaped stones occupied most of Leon's time. It was Betty, wiry, lissom, energy-charged, who did all the work and kept the nightclub from crashing onto the rocks. 'Leon has declared himself an artist,' she said of her husband. 'So now he refuses to be judged by ordinary standards and evades normal responsibilities.'

(Patience, patience. We are getting there.)

Betty Knut. Granddaughter of the Russian composer Alexander Scriabin, she had been, in her teenage years, active in the French Resistance and was awarded the Croix de Guerre. There were rumours that she'd been involved with the Zionist terrorist gang Lehi, better known as the Stern Gang. The rumours turned out to be true. In April 1947, Betty had beguiled her way into the Foreign and Colonial Office in London and planted a bomb in the toilet. Fortunately, a cleaner had discovered it before it could explode. A few months later she was arrested on the French-Belgian frontier carrying a suitcase packed with letter bombs addressed to members of the British cabinet. She was sentenced to a year in juvenile prison. Did she regret her terrorist activities? She never spoke of them.

By the way, two of Israel's prime ministers were leaders of terrorist gangs: Yitzhak Shamir (Lehi) and Menachem Begin (Irgun). And it was Lehi that offered to support the Nazis in 1940 in return for German support for a Jewish state in Palestine.

When Leon was absent, Betty would discard Mahalia and play records of her favourite: Georges Brassens. And that's where I first heard his name and his voice and his unremarkable guitar playing, though it made very little impression on me at the time.

So, wondering what 'a British Brassens' might sound like, I bought some of his recordings, a book of his lyrics in the series *Poètes d'Aujourd'hui*, and a French dictionary, essential for unravelling the meanings of his songs. The book's introduction informed me that some critics considered his songs shameless, an affront to good sense and good taste. I was won over immediately.

What particularly attracted me was that these songs were not folk songs, not pop songs, but belonged to a genre that didn't exist in England: chanson. They embraced the satirical with the sombre, the bawdy with the tender, the serious with the light-hearted. Their language mixed highly colloquial with poetic-literary, and they seemed to have been born into the world perfectly formed with never a botched rhyme. I was particularly drawn to the satirical antiwar 'La Guerre de 14–18,' which got him into trouble with veterans of the war, the anarchist-tinged 'La Mauvaise Reputation,' and the moving tribute to the couple who sheltered him during the war, 'L'Auvergnat.'

Some songs, though, I found so insubstantial as to be hardly worth the effort. I made an English version of one such song, 'Marinette,' rendering 'j'avais l'air d'un con' into the more decorous 'oh what a fool.' It was not a success.

In 1967, I was again compared to Brassens by another reviewer, Stephen Sedley: 'Melodically he doesn't have the punch of Brassens but as a poet and technician he outstrips him.' I accepted the compliment but doubted its accuracy.

I remember seeing Brassens in concert in December 1969 towards the end of his three-month sellout run at Bobino in Paris. Just think of that. A bloke with a guitar, a bass player, a chair, and an awful lot of words selling out a concert hall for three months. It boggles the mind. Because flamboyant he wasn't—he claimed that he'd never wanted to be on stage. Occasionally he would wander round the stage looking worried, but mostly he just stood there, one foot on a chair, guitar resting on his knee, an occasional flicker of a smile, and delivered song after song without, as far as I can remember, ever addressing a word to the audience who were listening with rapt attention. A nonperformer after my own heart. 'Je chante pour les oreilles, pas pour les yeux,' he said.

The contrast with Jacques Brel was stark, and not just because Brel had a big band accompaniment. Brel's concert at the Albert Hall in 1966, the only one he ever gave in Britain, lingers still in my memory. The intensity with which he delivered his songs was riveting. Every song was a mini-drama, projected through the inflexions of his voice, the movements of his hands and body, the expressions on his face. It was theatre. There was total involvement in the characters his songs created—the bigots, the timid and the old, the drunkard, the broken-hearted friend Jef, the dully respectable Flemish women, the feverish lover waiting for his Madeleine who will never come. It's said that he threw up before every concert.

Extraordinary to think that in 1954 Brel competed in the Grand Prix de la Chanson at Knokke-le-Zoute and finished twenty-seventh out of twenty-eight participants. How do you recover from a setback like that? 'Well, at least I didn't come last.'

In the feminist 1970s, Brassens came in for criticism because of the portrayal of women in his songs. He protested his innocence—'Pour moi, la femme est une déesse'—thus compounding the offence. Brassens belonged to a French male culture where women are necessary, if incomprehensible, but pals—'les copains'—always take first place. Yet for thirty years he was constant to his companion, Joha Heiman, and wrote for her the magnificent 'La Non-Demande en Mariage' ('I have the honour not to ask your hand in marriage').

When the feminist songwriter Anne Sylvestre skipped onto the scene in the late 1950s, she was labelled 'Brassens en jupon.' She was not pleased. I remember reading that she even preferred Brel's misogyny to the way Brassens portrayed women in his songs. That seems harsh on Brassens.

Compared to Brel he is an innocent. Women are portrayed in Brel's songs as *infidèles*, lacking in tenderness, treating love as a game, always demanding ('Serai seul a nouveau / Et tu m'auras perdu / Rien qu'en me voulant trop / Tu m'auras gaspillé'). The men in love with these women are humiliated, turned into fools, obsessives, led by the nose, almost deranged, like the protagonists of 'Ne Me Quitte Pas,' 'Mathilde,' 'Madeleine,' 'Titine,' 'Clara.' More shocking are the generalised attacks on women in songs like 'Les Filles et Les Chiens,' with its wicked wordplay and clear preference for the dogs, and 'Les Biches' ('Elles sont notre premier ennemi').

'Biches,' by the way, means 'does,' female deer. In Hebrew, if I remember rightly (a fifty-fifty chance, I'd say) it translates as 'ofarim.'

And that, by a strange coincidence, takes me back to 1959, just before I left Israel, when I moved to Haifa and worked for a short while with a young couple, Etty and Avraham Reichstadt. They took as their stage name Ha Ofarim. After I'd left, I heard that a song I'd helped them arrange, 'Sus Etz' (Wooden Horse), had become a hit in Israel. In 1968, Esther and Abi Ofarim topped the UK charts with their version of 'Cinderella Rockefella.' They'd come a long way. Esther Ofarim sang in the 1963 Eurovision Song Contest representing Switzerland. She came second. The last I heard, they were both, though divorced, living in Germany.

Isn't it ironic that when Israelis become sick and tired of living in Israel, their most favoured city, after New York, is Berlin? According to the *Times of Israel*, since 2000, thirty-three thousand Israelis have taken citizenship in the country that gave the world the death camps.

Yes, I know. This is all by the way, but look—by the way is how most of my life seems to have been lived so that now, in my eighties, I'm still trying to puzzle out what exactly I'm supposed to be doing here. According to Kurt Vonnegut, who attributes this insight to his son Mark: 'We are here to help each other get through this thing, whatever it is.' Is that why I've been writing songs for the last sixty years? To help us get through this thing, whatever it is?

Nowadays Anne Sylvestre is lauded as 'La grande dame de la chanson française.' Her songs, like 'Mariette et François,' 'Que Vous Êtes Beau,' and 'La Faute à Eve,' are a refreshing counterbalance to the relentlessly male view of the world of most French songwriters. Brel, Brassens, Ferré, the grand triumvirate of French chanson. Or, if you prefer, Brassens, Brel, Ferré. Whichever way, Leo Ferré always comes last. All I know for certain about Ferré is that he had a pet monkey called Pepée, and his wife killed it. Or had it killed. I was told this story by an Italian student who was interviewing me for something or other. His sympathies were with Ferré and the monkey. I wondered. I once saw in a French news-paper a photo of Ferré, his wife, and the monkey sitting round the dinner table. A happy little family. Or not. I wrote a song about it called (what else?) 'The Poet, the Wife and the Monkey.' Ferré wrote and recorded a lament for his dead monkey. He called it (what else?) 'Pepée.'

In 2007, I went to Sète, where Brassens was born and is buried, though sadly not on the beach so he could spend eternity on holiday, as he'd requested in his song 'Supplique pour Être Enterré à la Plage de Sète.' There is a whole building there, L'Espace Georges Brassens, dedicated to his life and works. Not bad for a bloke with a pipe and a moustache who put words to tunes.

When Brassens died in 1981, Jake Thackray (who *was* the British Brassens if anyone was) remarked that you couldn't see the joins in his songs, a tribute to the meticulous skill with which he crafted them—a skill largely lacking in the songs of most English-speaking songwriters. I admire him for that and honour him for his integrity, his dislike of authority, his indifference to money and possessions, and, above all, his passion for song, his determination to take the song form seriously, not for fame, not for money, but for love of the art itself.

Brassens was sixty when he died. Brel died in 1978, aged forty-nine. Ferré was seventy-six. Boris Vian, whose song 'Le Déserteur' I recorded on my first LP, was only thirty-nine. He had a heart attack while watching a film made from his pulp fiction novel *J'Irai Cracher sur Vos Tombes*. As film criticisms go, that's pretty damning. Vian was also a jazz trumpeter and wrote surrealist novels. In one of them, *L'Arrache-coeur* (Heart Snatcher), a mother is so terrified of harm coming to her children she locks them up in a cage. I wrote a song based on that scenario called 'My Daughter, My Son.' Betty Knut also died of a heart attack in 1965, thirty-seven years young. So it goes. Anne Sylvestre, who was almost exactly the same age as me and continued singing into her eighties, died in 2020 aged 86.

All those who spend their lives conjuring songs out of love and thin air have my respect. Even Leonard Cohen.

The Ghost of Georges Brassens

My head was full of cotton wool, my pen was full of bile
It was one of those days when everything's grey and
*   nothing seems worthwhile*
The radio played the sort of crap that music hacks acclaim
I don't know why they call them songs, they don't deserve
*   the name*
And so I vowed I'd never write another song when
*   something weird*
Occurred and out of the dusty air a ghostly shape
*   appeared*
And I heard myself exclaiming Mon Dieu! Zut alors! et
    Mince!
I know that pipe and that moustache, it's the ghost of
*   Georges Brassens.*
I said, Georges, what are you doing here? I've seen your
*   grave in Sète.*

He said, I've come to tell you that you shouldn't give up yet.
It's all very well for you, Georges, your songs brought you
    fame
You sold a multitude of records, and all France knew your
    name.
He said, Until the age of 31 I never earned a cent
I remember the very first cheque I got I didn't know what
    it meant
I never wrote for money, and I never wanted fame
And if my songs had never earned a sou I'd have written
    them just the same …
You know for me to be in the public eye was always an
    ordeal
The trappings of celebrity for me had no appeal
My needs were few, for years I lived on little more than
    bread and cheese
In the world of fame and fashion I could not feel at ease.
This lust for money and possessions hasn't done the world
    much good
For myself I always tried to earn as little as I could.
Friendship, les copains, that's what mattered in the end
And the thing that I'm most proud of is I never lost a
    friend …
The thing is, Georges, I said, my songs have sometimes
    caused offence to Christians, royalists, Zionists,
    coppers, and others too numerous to list.
Et alors! he shrugged, some critics called my songs
    debased
Unpatriotic, sacrilegious, and in execrable taste.
They didn't like the way my songs debunked authority
The law, the church, the military, and la gendarmerie.
I lived my life, I wrote my songs, the way I wanted to
And if les braves gens disapproved, I told them, Je m'en
    fous …

For me song has a value that money cannot buy
For songs have been my passion, the salvation of my life
The songs that I created were a gift that I could share
And I would not cheat the public, so I crafted them with
    care
I chose the best and brightest words and taught them how
    to dance
I tried out many tunes to find the one that would enhance
the words. I laboured long and hard to polish, shape,
    refine
Every rhyme and every stanza, every bar and every line
And by the way that tune you're singing sounds like one of
    mine.
I died too soon with many songs unborn, and that's my
    one regret
Remember that, he said, and now I must return to Sète.
Merci, I said, it's always good communing with the dead
And the lyrics of this song began revolving in my head.

5

Sing a Song of Politics

*Give me the making of the songs of a nation and I care
not who makes its laws.*

—Andrew Fletcher (1655–1716)

In 1981, David Widgery, a leading light in the Trotskyist
Socialist Workers Party, wrote an article in *New Socialist*
called, if I remember rightly, 'The Rocky Road to Socialism.'
In it he pronounced the folk idiom well and truly dead
and proclaimed rock music as the true road to revolution.
The argument went like this: a socialist movement needs
a culture for its emotional appeal and, if it is ever to be
a mass movement, it needs a mass culture so that it can
mobilise people who have no interest in political ideology.
Rock music is that mass culture (that was then). Therefore
true socialists must march along the road to revolution in
time to the sound of rock. And if you weren't persuaded
by his reasoning, a quotation from authority figures like
Vladimir Lenin and Walter Benjamin, now rocking away
in the other world, should put you in your place. German
socialist artists like Brecht, Heartfield, and Piscator are
rapped on the knuckles by Widgery for failing to halt the
rise of fascism, while Hitler gets full marks for his 'brilliance
at cultural and emotional manipulation—*soul massage*—as
Goebbels called it.'

His article is more than a desperate plea by a terminally frustrated revolutionary. Yes, it is opportunistic, ignores the transitory nature of popular commercial music, sees the fans, who are passionate about this music, and the rock bands as pawns to be manipulated in the service of a political agenda:

THE CAPITALIST SYSTEM WAS TODAY OVERTHROWN BY BERT GOEBBELS AND THE SOUL MASSEURS, A FUNKY ROCK GROUP, IN SYMBIOTIC RELATIONSHIP WITH THE LEFT. BERT HIMSELF ADMITTED TO BEING SURPRISED BY THIS OUTCOME AND SAID MODESTLY THAT ALL THEY WERE REALLY TRYING TO DO WAS MAKE THE CHARTS.

Nevertheless, it makes many valid points: ' "Our Great Movement" has very nearly succeeded in boring a generation to political death by its narrow definitions of what is political, its enslavement to institutional ritual and its lack of skill and cultural variety in communicating its ideas.' It is also a perfect illustration of a long-held belief on the left and in vanguard parties that music, song can be, should be a political weapon to rally the working class, the masses, to bring about a better society, to change the world. No doubt the Left has all the best songs but, given the state of the world and the working classes, it's an assumption we should treat with some caution.

Widgery's article is, in a sense, Trotsky versus Stalin, round 99: Music. The Communist Party, after all, had cornered the market in folk music. Or so Widgery believed. Hence his dismissal of folk as 'deliberately doleful,' 'pre-electronic,' and no longer relevant. In the 1930s in the United States, the Communist Party argued with itself as to whether workers' choirs or some ill-defined thing called folk music was the likelier to lead the working class to the barricades. The model for workers' choirs came from Weimar, Germany, where Hanns Eisler, a highly sophisticated composer who had studied with Schoenberg, sought to change the world through music. He set didactic texts to music for workers' choral societies to sing and wrote, with fellow communist Bertolt Brecht, *Kampflieder*, fighting songs, like 'Song of the United Front' and 'Solidarity Song,' whose purpose was to raise consciousness and create workers' solidarity.

'The task of workers' music will be to remove the sentimentality and pompousness from music, since these sensations divert us from the class struggle,' Eisler asserted. In the end, of course, the Communist Party USA decreed that folk music was indeed the music of the people, even though it clearly wasn't. This decision led to an upsurge of politically conscious 'folk songs' and, at the end of the 1930s, to the formation of the Almanac Singers, which included Woody Guthrie and Pete Seeger, whose professed aim was to 'make and sing songs however and whenever they are needed in the workers' struggle.' This, it should be made clear, was the workers' struggle as defined by the Communist Party, which meant that when Hitler attacked the Soviet Union and the war became a People's War, the Almanacs dropped their anti-war songs and started singing anti-Hitler songs instead, and when the party agreed to a no-strike clause, union songs like 'Talking Union' were junked. This occasioned much merriment and satirical comment among other left-wing groups.

In any event, the barricades remained unbuilt, and when the mass popularity of radical folk song came about in the 1960s it resulted not from working-class militancy but from the disaffection of middle-class youth. It is arguable how much effect those songs that reflected and energised the youth rebellion of that decade had on political change. They flourished for a time both at the grass roots and, in a soft-centred form, in the marketplace, at least until the market rendered them obsolete. The commercial music machine after all had no problem in absorbing, filtering out, and repackaging the folk-protest songs of the early sixties and the hippie counterculture music of the West Coast rock bands in the late sixties. The sound of rebellion turned out to be as saleable as any other sound.

By the 1970s and 1980s, the idea that folk song was going to overthrow the capitalist system was looking decidedly quaint. In 1986, the history professor Jesse Lemisch followed the Widgery line by launching a scathing attack in the left-wing magazine *The Nation* on the Left's espousal of, as he put it, 'the archaic aesthetic of the folk world,' singling out Pete Seeger and Si Kahn for what he called their inauthenticity. To reach the masses, Lemisch argued, the Left had to embrace mass-market music.

In Britain, too, the Communist Party espoused folk song as the music that would enthuse the people with a vision of a different sort of world. Ewan MacColl and A.L. Lloyd, two of the begetters of the 1950s folk revival, were both, at that time, Communist Party members. Folk clubs proliferated, many with a leftist political agenda, and new songs were written in the folk form, at a time when the grip by the professionals on commercial music had yet to be loosened, and were the accompaniment to various political campaigns, especially CND and the Aldermaston marches.

In the late 1970s, the debate around music and politics reached fever pitch. Or at least became moderately heated. It even infiltrated the academic world in a book called *Media, Politics and Culture: A Socialist View* (Macmillan, 1979) to which I contributed a chapter. Should socialist musicians (and cultural workers generally) work in the mass media and the marketplace to reach the maximum number of people—or outside so as not to lose control of their art?

In 1977, Music for Socialism was formed, a diverse group of musicians whose aim, like the Almanacs, was 'to place our capabilities at the service of the struggle of the working class towards socialism.' But as to the sort of music that would bring about that happy outcome, on that there was no agreement. I have a vivid memory of the Music for Socialism Festival held in Battersea Arts Centre. The performers represented the whole spectrum of 'radical' music, from the hard-line marching songs of People's Liberation Music (PLM), the musical arm of a Maoist group, led by Cornelius Cardew, once famous for his avant-garde experimental compositions, to acoustic songwriters like me, to the free-form hippyish jazz group Red Balune, which featured a man dressed as a janitor playing a broom (making a sweeping statement, as the *Times* review wittily commented). Though self-defined as socialist, we had nothing in common musically or politically. After each concert, the audience members were invited to voice their criticisms of the performers. A splendid idea, I think. The critical terms used were perhaps not very subtle but they were passionately felt. 'Anarchist wanker,' they charged. 'Bourgeois sellout.' PLM were accused of being 'militaristic robots.' 'Bourgeois bollocks,' I remember, was aimed at the avant-garde group Henry Cow, who took a strongly anti-populist line. Radical politics, they said, had to have a radical language. They objected to Rock Against Racism. To settle for progressive content in a reactionary form marks a real collapse in contemporary art culture, they said. Form and content must advance together. Revolutionary content demands revolutionary form. Listening to Henry Cow and its offshoot Art Bears was a genuinely weird experience.

And then there was punk rock, and that was going to challenge the establishment and Red Wedge was going to convince the youth to put their trust in Kinnock, except it didn't. There are limits to the power of song. Songs can cement people's beliefs. They can't change them. Solidarity songs are great for bringing people together in a common cause, for making a community of the already converted, but they don't do much for the unconverted. I don't believe that political commitment, let alone understanding, comes about in a flash of musical light nor that ingrained beliefs and prejudices and conditioning and attitudes born of every-day experience can be magically transformed by listening to songs, least of all to songs that simply make statements, rhyme arguments, or chant slogans.

The debate that has raged over the years about which is the right music to rouse the masses seems now to have no relevance. Widgery's argument depended largely on the success of Rock Against Racism. But rock only works in certain contexts, in large spaces and in the marketplace, and it works almost exclusively for one age group. It communicates through sounds, repetition, and volume rather than words, it gives the hearers no space to think for themselves and allows little room for subtlety, humour, irony, thoughtfulness. As for the Widgery/Lemisch argument that a mass movement needs a mass culture, which means whatever music is selling in the marketplace, that, in my view, completely misunder-stands how commercial music is transmitted and received. The industry that turns people into consumers and music into a product for leisure-time consumption functions like any other capitalist industry. Record companies, publishers, agents, and managers invest in a product and expect to see a return on that investment. A group that fails to achieve an adequate return is made redundant. Market forces rule. The music, in any case, is only a part of the package. And the message of the medium is that the words don't matter. The image matters, the style, the clothes, the charisma, the sound, the beat, the mode of performance, the outward show—these matter. Any significance the words may attempt to carry is inevitably undermined by the medium through which it is transmitted.

'For me the words are just a carefully manufactured part of the packaging medium of the music,' Frank Zappa said. 'The words are more relevant to the album cover than they are to the songs.'

In 2008, David Cameron, British prime minister, declared his liking for the Jam's songs in general and 'Eton Rifles' in particular. Since 'Eton Rifles' was supposed to be an attack on class privilege, this seemed puzzling. 'Is nothing sacred?' asked the *Guardian*'s John Harris. Paul Weller was bemused. 'He must have an idea what it's about, surely. It's a shame really that someone didn't listen to that song and get something else from it and become a socialist leader instead. I was a bit disappointed really.' Yes, if only Cameron had really listened to the words, he could have become the first social-ist leader of the Conservative Party. Of course, he heard the words and knew what it was about. But in that context, what are words, anyway? Just part of the package, aren't they? 'I don't see why the left should be the only ones allowed to listen to protest songs,' Cameron said. What strains credulity even more is that Ed Vaizey, another Tory MP who loved the Jam and had seen them play, admitted a fondness for the Redskins who were the Socialist Workers Party's favourite band. What would Widgery have said about that?

Song is an infinitely flexible form, and there are ways of challenging the status quo in song without telling people what to think and what to do. Songs don't have to divide audiences into believers and non-believers. Songs are at their most interesting and are most likely to reach 'nonpolitical' audiences if they have at their heart not issues, messages, or abstractions but people, if they tell stories rather than transmit slogans, if they find the political in the personal (and the other way around), if they communicate through words rather than sounds, if they ask questions rather than give answers, if they grant audiences space to make up their own minds, if they allow room for humour, humanity, wit, subtlety, and imagination. Because most people don't live their lives on the barricades and, as Jesse Lemisch asks, 'If the left aims only at the didactic, who will chart the human soul?'

6

Stand Up for Judas

I wrote 'Stand Up for Judas' sometime in the 1970s. I knew it would be controversial (to put it mildly) and get me into any number of fruitless arguments. So what prompted me write it?

Here's the story. I was walking down the Harrow Road in a dreary part of London one bleak December day when I passed a church. A large placard outside caught my eye. On it was written in dramatically bold letters: IF YOU BELIEVE NOT THAT I AM THE CHRIST YOU SHALL DIE IN YOUR SINS (JOHN 8:24).

For some reason I felt indignant. Not that being in or out of my sins when I'm dying concerns me but this seemed so presumptuous. Who was this cocksure Jewish preacher to make such an assertion? And how come so many groups and people of such different—even opposing—persuasions claim to follow Jesus' teachings? How can liberation theologians and evangelical Christians, supporters of apartheid in South Africa and opponents of it, Ronald Reagan and Martin Luther King Jr., Bruce Kent and Tony Blair, all cite the Jesus we only know from the gospels as their moral guide?

So I found a dilapidated Holy Bible—a family heir-loom ('translated out of the original tongues; and with the former translations diligently compared and revised, by His Majesty's special command')—and set about reading. I read from 'The book of the generation of Jesus Christ' in Matthew to the final 'Amen' in John.

These were my first thoughts:

There are contradictions and inconsistencies in the portrait of Jesus that make it impossible to assemble him as a coherent figure. There isn't one Jesus. For example, there's the nonviolent Jesus in Matthew who reproves the disciples for fighting back when he is arrested: 'All they that take the sword shall perish by the sword.' And there's the violent Jesus in Luke who tells these same disciples to sell their garments and buy swords: 'And they said, Lord, behold, there are two swords. And he said unto them, it is enough.' There's the Jesus who said, 'Resist not evil,' and the Jesus who said, 'I came not to bring peace but a sword.' This explains why even opposing viewpoints can find some evidence for the Jesus they believe in.

The gospel Jesus may have shown charitable feelings towards the poor but he had no interest in liberating them from their misery ('Ye have the poor always with you') or in changing an unjust world. He accepted the status quo because he was a divinity whose kingship was not of this world.

The gospels are anti-Jewish. The Jews are made responsible for Jesus' crucifixion: 'His blood be on us, and on our children' (Matthew 27:25). Inexplicably, those same Jews calling for Jesus' crucifixion on the Friday had, only five days earlier, acclaimed him as the son of David and, because of their support, prevented the authorities from arresting him (Matthew 21:46). In John's gospel, the enemies of Jesus are no longer the Pharisees but the Jews. Jesus has become a non-Jew. And since only those who believe in Christ's divinity can be saved, Jews, non-believers, are cast into hell. 'He that believeth and is baptised shall be saved; but he that believeth not shall be damned' (Mark 16:16).

And then there's the choice of Judas—meaning Jew—to be the disciple who betrays Jesus.

Centuries of antisemitism and persecution have their origin in the writings of the gospel makers.

After that, I read Hyam Maccoby's book *Revolution in Judaea* and tried to find out more about the historical context in which this charismatic Jewish preacher was working his miracles.

The most obvious historical fact is that Judaea, Galilee, and Samaria were occupied territories. The Roman occupation was cruel, rapacious, and corrupt. It was marked by Jewish uprisings (Barabbas is said to have been involved in one such uprising) which were mercilessly crushed by the Romans with crucifixion as the common punishment. In 6 CE when, according to the experts, Jesus would have been about twelve, there was a census of the inhabitants of Judaea and Samaria which provoked a rebellion led by a rabbi called Judas of Galilee who founded the Zealot party. Josephus, the renegade Jewish historian (37 CE to circa 100), wrote of the Zealots: 'These men have an inviolable attachment to liberty and say that God is to be their only Ruler and Lord.'

The Romans imposed heavy taxes on the mass of Jewish smallholders and landless labourers. Tax collection was contracted out to 'publicans,' as they are called in the New Testament, who wanted their cut and who could be ruthless and violent to those who couldn't afford to pay. They were often Jews who were hated and despised for their extortionate acts and for collaborating with the occupation. 'The Romans deliberately choose as tax collectors men who are absolutely ruthless and savage and give them the means of satisfying their greed.... They exact money not only from people's property but also from their bodies by means of personal injuries, assault and completely unheard forms of torture' (Philo 25 BCE to 50 CE, *De Specialibus Legibus*).

So what does the gospel Jesus have to say about this brutal oppression of his people? Almost nothing. Remarkably, there is no mention in the gospels of the Roman occupation.

Jesus is pictured as being in conflict not with the Roman rulers but with the mainstream Jewish party, the Pharisees. Jesus only mentions the Romans once: 'Render unto Caesar the things that are Caesar's and unto God the things that are God's.' An injunction against the nonviolent resistance of a tax strike. This is not credible. It is like setting a story in today's Palestine without mentioning Israel's brutal occupation. Who would do that?

Equally ahistorical is the way Pilate is portrayed: mild, well-meaning, indecisive, and weak, perhaps, but ultimately not responsible for Jesus' crucifixion. The real Pilate was nothing like that. Between 16 CE and 26 CE there were four procurators, all of them corrupt and rapacious. Pontius Pilate was appointed procurator in 26 CE and is considered the worst of them all. According to Philo, 'He was cruel by nature and hard-hearted and entirely lacking in remorse.' Philo describes his rule as consisting of 'bribes, vainglorious and insolent conduct, robbery, oppression, humiliations, men sent to death untried and incessant and unmitigated cruelty.'

Josephus describes Pilate as deliberately seeking to outrage the religious feelings of the Jews by marching his army of occupation from Caesarea to the Holy City, with their standards containing images of Tiberius as a god in order to abolish the Jewish laws.

Pilate was eventually deposed and sent to Rome in 37 CE for harshly suppressing a Samaritan movement.

Furthermore, Jesus is described as being in perpetual conflict with the Pharisees, who are in league with the Sadducees and Herodians. But this makes no sense since the Pharisees and Sadducees were on opposing sides. The Sadducees were collaborators who supported the status quo and accepted official posts under the Romans and the Herodians. They were the party of the rich landowners and priestly families. The High Priest was a Sadducee appointed by Rome. The Pharisees were the mainstream religious party, representing the mass of the people from small landowners to peasants and craftsmen. In matters of doctrine, they had fundamental differences with the Sadducees. The Sadducees were traditionalists who believed the Torah was cast in stone. The Pharisees, on the other hand, argued that the Torah was a living thing that could be supplemented and developed into oral law. The place of the Torah was 'not in heaven but in the hands of men.' 'The Pharisees have delivered to the people a great many observances by succession from their fathers which are not written in the laws of Moses,' Josephus wrote, 'and it is for this reason that the Sadducees reject them.'

So it's clear that the gospels are a deliberate distortion of history; they are anti-Jewish, pro-Roman propaganda. This is not surprising when you consider who the gospel makers were and when the gospels were written. Mark, Matthew, Luke, and John. None of them knew Jesus; all of them lived outside Palestine; their culture was Hellenist. Mark is the earliest, around 70 CE, John the latest, around 100 CE. All, then, were written after the great Jewish revolt against the Roman occupation.

This started as a tax strike in 66 CE, led by the Zealots, and escalated into a full-blown rebellion. The Romans were driven out of Jerusalem. Rome's Syrian Legion was ambushed and defeated by Jewish rebels at the Battle of Beth Horon, with six thousand Romans massacred. But eventually the Roman army prevailed, the uprising was crushed, and in 70 CE, after a seven-month siege, Jerusalem was taken and the Second Temple destroyed. According to Titus Flavius Josephus—who by that time had defected to the Romans and changed his name from Yosef ben Matityahu—over a million noncombatants died, thousands were crucified, and thousands more enslaved.

Understandably, this revolt against Rome did not make Jews popular in the various countries of the Roman Empire in which they lived. And at this time of intense anti-Jewish feeling it would have been imprudent, not to say dangerous, for the gospels to dwell on the brutality of Roman rule (better ignore it completely) or to portray the Jews in a positive light.

What historical evidence is there for the existence of Jesus? Not a lot. One, maybe two mentions in Josephus. And scholars speculate that there was an original gospel, now lost and written closer to Jesus' lifetime, which was the source of Matthew, Mark, and Luke and that different bits of that original account survive in their versions. That would explain some of the contradictions in the gospel stories. In any case, at that time of oppression, misery, defeat, and despair, it is highly likely that messianic preachers would arise, gaining a following by promising hope and deliverance, and that fabulous stories would be told about their miraculous powers. Perhaps the militant Jesus who ordered his followers to buy swords was the real Jesus. But this is speculation. In the end, the gospel Jesus is the only Jesus we have, and he is certainly the Jesus of Saint Paul and the mainstream Christian church. My song puts him into his historical times and finds him wanting. Each verse is based on Jesus' actual deeds and teachings in the gospels. The last two lines are the point of the song.

The title of the song 'Stand up for Judas' is deliberately provocative since it not only references and challenges the hymn 'Stand Up, Stand Up for Jesus' but also upends the image of Judas Iscariot as the very embodiment of venality and betrayal. Iscariot is derived from 'sicarius,' meaning dagger-man or assassin. The Sicarii were the most militant of the Zealot party, and the Zealots were the militant wing of the Pharisees. They believed in open resistance to Roman rule and that God would come to their aid but only if they showed zeal, like Phineas the Zealot in Numbers 25. So, in the song, Judas the Zealot is the voice of the resistance and a critic of the passivity of Jesus in the face of oppression.

One May Day in the early nineties I gave a concert in Catholic Belfast. To my amazement I was asked if I would sing 'Stand Up for Judas.' So I did. Nervously. Apparently the IRA, or some members of it, identified with Judas as a hero of the resistance.

It's been recorded by Roy Bailey, David Campbell, and Dick Gaughan and sung in concerts around the country, including at least one church.

> *We sang in church* 'Stand Up for Judas'
> *Nobody left, nobody booed us.*
> *Our thankful timbers stayed unshivered*
> *His thunderbolts went undelivered.*
> *Applause was all that rattled in those*
> *Hallowed walls and stained-glass windows.*
> *Who knows what hellfire—and who cares?—*
> *Ascended with the rector's prayers.*

As far as I know it's never been played on any radio programme in England. No surprise there. It was played on CBC, in Canada, and prompted an immediate angry letter demanding that 'this blasphemous song' should never be aired. But I don't think it is blasphemous. The Catholic Workers in Baltimore heard it with interest and found it serious enough to discuss. Played on KPFA in Berkeley, it acquired a following. The main accusation against the song has been that the song's Jesus is a caricature, 'not the real Jesus.' A fellow songwriter claimed that I was relying too much on the gospel of John. 'Compare the more historical gospel of Mark with John,' he wrote, 'and you find you are reading about two completely different people.' Well, exactly.

As the environmental writer Paul Harrison has written: 'Christ can be used, and has been used, as a motivation for total self-sacrifice to bring about justice on earth, or for giving 0.01 per cent of one's annual income to Oxfam or the NSPCC. As an inspiration to die resisting tyranny or to turn the other cheek to oppression; to take up arms for socialism, or against it. The truth is that humans have to decide for themselves what kind of society is best and how to achieve it. The gospels, unfortunately—or fortunately—don't provide a lot of help. We're on our own.'

> The Romans were the masters when Jesus walked the land
> In Judaea and in Galilee they ruled with an iron hand.
> The poor were sick with hunger and the rich were clothed
>   in splendour
> And the rebels whipped and crucified hung rotting as a
>   warning.
> And Jesus knew the answer
> Said, Give to Caesar what is Caesar's
> Said, Love your enemies
> But Judas was a Zealot, and he wanted to be free.
> Resist, he said, the Romans' tyranny.
> So stand up, stand up for Judas and the cause that Judas
>   served
> It was Jesus who betrayed the poor with his word.
> Jesus was a conjuror, miracles were his game
> And he fed the hungry thousands and they glorified his
>   name.
> He cured the lame and the leper. He calmed the wind and
>   the weather.
> And the wretched flocked to touch him so their troubles
>   would be taken.
> And Jesus knew the answer.
> All you who labour, all you who suffer
> Only believe in me.
> But Judas sought a world where no one starved or begged
>   for bread.
> The poor are always with us, Jesus said.
> So stand up, stand up …
> Jesus brought division where none had been before
> Not the slaves against their masters but the poor against
>   the poor.

Set son to rise up against father, and brother to fight
        against brother
For he that is not with me is against me was his teaching.
Said Jesus, I am the answer,
You unbelievers shall burn forever
Shall die in your sins.
Not sheep and goats, said Judas, but together we may dare
Shake off the chains of misery we share.
So stand up, stand up …
Jesus stood upon the mountain with a distance in his eyes.
I am the way, the life, he cried, the light that never dies.
So renounce all earthly treasures and pray to your
        heavenly Father
And he pacified the hopeless with the hope of life eternal.
Said Jesus, I am the answer
All you who hunger, only remember
Your reward's in heaven.
So Jesus preached the other world, but Judas wanted this
And he betrayed his master with a kiss.
So stand up, stand up …
By sword and gun and crucifix, Christ's gospel has been
        spread
And two thousand cruel years have shown the way that
        Jesus led.
The heretics burned and tortured, the butchering bloody
        crusaders.
The bombs and rockets sanctified that rained down death
        from heaven.
They followed Jesus. They knew the answer.
All non-believers must be believers
Or else be broken.
So put no trust in saviours, Judas said, for everyone
Must be to his or her own self a sun.

7

Beware! It Is Catching and Can Rot Your Brain

Experts say that it is rarely fatal but can cause many unpleasant symptoms including brain rot, selective vision, and moral turpitude. I am referring, of course, to *zionusitis*, a disease that has become increasingly fashionable in these grim times.

An outbreak of *zionusitis* occurred recently on a Virgin Atlantic airline when passengers were forced to confront a menu that included the item 'Palestinian couscous salad.' Those who harboured the *zionusitis* virus were immediately reduced to gibbering wrecks. Some fainted clean away while one man clutched his head and called out again and again, 'Oi va voi li!'—which airline staff interpreted as a spell to ward off the evil spirits. Investigations confirmed that the spark that set off this explosion of inanity was not the word 'salad' or the word 'couscous' but the P word. The highly contagious nature of this sickness is evidenced by the fact that the boss of Virgin, Sir Richard Branson, though he had had no direct personal contact with these poor unfortunates, almost immediately succumbed to a nasty attack of moral turpitude and deleted the offending word from the menu.

Curiously enough, this is not the first time an item of food has been responsible for a *zionusitis* happening. In July 2014, an elderly Jewish couple misheard the word 'hummus' as 'Hamas' and fled screaming from the restaurant.

Along with paranoid hysteria, those who suffer from this disease often exhibit a symptom experts call 'reality disconnect,' whereby they are overtaken by delusions and fantasies which lead them to see things that aren't there— antisemitism, for example. Typically, they will then indulge in an orgy of finger-jabbing and wild accusations, although whether this behaviour is genuinely felt or is simply a way of calling attention to themselves is never entirely clear.

A virulent strain of this disease is particularly prevalent among Labour MPs, including members of the shadow cabinet. Having become infected, they will intone, over and over again, the words 'peace-process-two-state-solution, peace-process-two-state-solution' until challenged as to the meaning of this mysterious mantra, when they will clap their hands over their ears and sing out 'Na-na-na-na-na can't hear you' before collapsing in a catatonic heap.

Many experts argue that, once contracted, *zionusitis* is incurable, but there have been cases where a healthy dose of reality administered three times daily for six months has effected a remarkable recovery.

The source of this illness has been traced to a small self-styled democracy somewhere in the Middle East which calls itself Israel and claims to be Jewish. Whatever that means.

8

Welcome to the Witch Hunt

My local Labour-controlled council has just voted, like other councils, as well as universities and the UK government, to adopt the International Holocaust Remembrance Alliance (IHRA) definition of antisemitism. This consists of a rather loose basic definition, followed by a rambling discourse around the subject that twice mentions Israel and then examples, seven of which refer to the state of Israel. Anyone with a functioning brain might suspect that this definition has less to do with protecting Jews from antisemitism than with shielding Israel from criticism.

When the European Parliament was due to vote on whether to adopt this definition, I wrote to my MEPs urging them to reject it. Two replied in identical terms, pointing out that the definition makes it clear that 'criticism of Israel cannot be regarded as antisemitic.' Except that it doesn't. They lied. Why would they do that? What it actually says is that 'criticism of Israel *similar to that levelled against any other country* cannot be regarded as antisemitic.'

The italicised phrase changes everything. Why is it there? Obviously to muddy the waters. Who is to decide whether criticism of Israel goes beyond that levelled against any other country? In any case, Israel is not like any other country. It is a settler colonial state, founded on massacres and ethnic cleansing. It is, by any definition, a criminal state.

Transferring Israeli settlers into the occupied territory is illegal, as is transferring Palestinian prisoners into Israeli jails. The wall, built largely on Palestinian land, was judged illegal by the International Court of Justice in 2004. The collective punishment inflicted on the people of Gaza is a war crime under the Fourth Geneva Convention. Israel itself is a racist state where 'Arabs' are viewed as a demographic threat. Unlike other countries (Myanmar is an exception), it is not a state for all its citizens but for all the Jews in the world, who are given the 'Right of Return,' a right denied to the indigenous people.

But according to the IHRA definition we are not allowed to say this. What makes Israel worthy of special protection?

The IHRA definition gives as an example of antisemitism: 'Denying the Jewish people their right to self-determination, e.g. by claiming that the existence of Israel is a racist endeavour.'

This is tantamount to saying that antisemitism is the same as anti-Zionism since only Zionists (and antisemites) believe that Jews are 'a people' and that their self-determination means a Jewish state. Jews are not, in any ethnic sense, a people or a race. All that Jews share is a religion—and whatever ethical values may be derived from that—and a history of persecution. The mass of Yiddish-speaking Jews in Poland, Lithuania, and Russia were against the Zionist project. True, the socialist Bund wanted Jewish autonomy based on a language and a culture, for which they were labelled 'Zionists with seasickness' by someone (probably Lenin), but they were totally opposed to a Jewish state in Palestine. So were the religious authorities of the time since it is written in the Torah and the Talmud that Jews are forbidden to return to the Holy Land until the Messiah comes. Nowadays most Jewish religious groupings have accommodated themselves to the reality of the Jewish state even though it would seem to be a sin against God.

Many prominent Jews opposed the 1917 Balfour Declaration, notably Edwin Montagu, the only Jewish member of the cabinet. He considered Zionism a form of antisemitism. He was not alone. Members of the mainstream Board of Deputies of British Jews, like Lucien Wolf and Alexander Montefiore, argued fervently against the idea of a Jewish state since inherent in the Zionist project is the belief that Jews do not belong in the countries where they have lived over the centuries, that they are 'strangers in their native lands.'

Judah Magnes (the first president of the Hebrew University, who lobbied US president Harry Truman not to recognise the state of Israel), biblical scholar Martin Buber and philosopher and political theorist Hannah Arendt (both refugees from Nazi Germany), and Albert Einstein were all sympathetic to the idea of a Jewish homeland in Palestine but firmly opposed to a Jewish state because they understood that it would necessarily displace the Arab population of Palestine. They favoured a binational state with equal rights for all. In Einstein's evidence to the Anglo-American Committee of Inquiry, which was examining the Palestine issue in 1946, Einstein argued against the creation of a Jewish state. 'The state idea is not according to my heart. I cannot understand why it is needed. It is connected with many difficulties and narrow-mindedness. I believe it is bad.... I am against it.'

After Israel's creation, he wrote: 'My awareness of the essential nature of Judaism resists the idea of a Jewish state with borders, an army, and a measure of temporal power, no matter how modest.'

Now, according to the IHRA definition, all these and countless more, including many Israelis such as the academics Shlomo Sand, Ilan Pappé, and Moshe Machover, are guilty of antisemitism. Isn't it absurd? Yet councillors all over the country as well as university authorities have been mindlessly voting to adopt this pernicious definition.

Another example of antisemitism given in the definition is: 'Drawing comparisons of contemporary Israeli policy to that of the Nazis.' In what way is that antisemitic? And if there is evidence for such comparisons, why are we not allowed to say so?

Hannah Arendt, in her book *Eichmann in Jerusalem*, notes the parallels between the Nazi Nuremberg Laws of 1935, which prohibit intermarriage between Jews and Germans, and Israel's own marriage laws, where, because rabbinical law rules, 'no Jew can marry a non-Jew.' So now she's guilty of antisemitism twice over.

In 2014, with Israel's onslaught on Gaza at its height, I wrote a song, 'The Ballad of Rivka and Mohammed,' which drew parallels between the experience of a Jewish girl in the Vilna Ghetto and a Palestinian boy in Gaza. That would undoubtedly have fallen foul of this clause in the definition and got me suspended from the Labour Party, had I been a member.

In March 2017, a Jewish Holocaust survivor, Marika Sherwood, was due to give an open talk at Manchester University, with the title 'A Holocaust Survivor's Story and the Balfour Declaration: You're Doing to the Palestinians What the Nazis Did to Me.'

I don't know what exactly she had in mind when choosing that title. She did say in explanation: 'I was just speaking of my experience of what the Nazis were doing to me as a Jewish child. I had to move away from where I was living because Jews couldn't live there.... I can't say I'm a Palestinian, but my experiences as a child are not dissimilar to what Palestinian children are experiencing now.'

Perhaps she was thinking of how Israeli soldiers routinely invade Palestinian homes in the middle of the night, drag out young boys, handcuff and blindfold them, beat them, humiliate and abuse them, deny them access to family or a lawyer, and then hold them in physically abusive conditions, tied to a chair, for example, until they sign confessions—stone-throwing is a typical accusation—in a language they don't understand. The maximum sentence for throwing stones is twenty years.

'Israel has the dubious distinction of being the only country in the world that systematically prosecutes between 500 and 700 children each year in military courts lacking fundamental fair trial rights,' says Defense for Children International–Palestine. 'Children within the Israeli military system commonly report physical and verbal abuse from the moment of their arrest, and coercion and threats during interrogations.' The UN Committee on the Rights of the Child reports: 'Palestinian children arrested by (Israeli) military and police are systematically subject to degrading treatment, and often to acts of torture, are interrogated in Hebrew, a language they did not understand, and sign confessions in Hebrew in order to be released.'

Of course, there was no antisemitic intent in her choice of title. But after pressure from the Israeli embassy (Mark Regev, the Israeli ambassador to the UK, was formerly Israel's minister of propaganda—they call it 'hasbara' in Hebrew—and was often referred to as Israel's Goebbels), the university insisted the subtitle be removed, that academics chosen to chair the meeting be replaced by university appointees, and that attendance be limited to university students and staff.

The embassy argued that 'comparing Israel to the Nazi regime could reasonably be considered antisemitic, given the context, according to IHRA's working definition of antisemitism.'

And this, of course, is what it's all about. Silencing, censoring, stifling legitimate free speech. Nothing to do with combatting real antisemitism, everything to do with false accusations of antisemitism to protect Israel from criticism. The IHRA definition has been used as an excuse to suspend or expel too many Labour Party members, to close down too many meetings supporting Palestinian rights, to smear with spurious accusations of antisemitism too many speakers and writers speaking out for justice for Palestinians. Professor Moshe Machover is just the latest example, expelled from the Labour Party for writing an article in the Labour Party Marxists' newsletter which documents the collaboration between the Nazi regime and the Zionist movement. The accuracy of his article has, unsurprisingly, not been challenged since it is all a matter of historical record. But the expulsion letter maintains that his article 'appears to meet the International Holocaust Remembrance Alliance definition of antisemitism which has been adopted by the Labour Party.' In fact, the Labour Party has wisely not adopted the whole definition, only the basic working definition without the examples, and it is difficult to understand how anything in Machover's article could be construed as antisemitic on that basis. But any excuse . . .

The letter also mentions, as an affront to the etiquette of the Labour Party, 'language that could be perceived as offensive.' That is a common charge made by the Zionist Jewish Labour Movement. They are offended if you call Israel a criminal state, they are offended if you label Israel's policies as racist, and they are offended if you mention apartheid when referring to the occupation. They are sensitive souls and are easily offended, and since they are offended and they are Jews, you must be antisemitic.

Well, tough. There is not, as far as I know, a human right not to be offended. I am offended by the machinations of the Zionist lobby. I am offended by the *Daily Mail*, the *Sun*, the *Times*, and the *Telegraph*. I am offended by Boris Johnson and the toff with six offspring who loves food banks. I am offended by Israel claiming to speak for me. I am offended every time Netanyahu opens his mouth. I am particularly offended by being accused of antisemitism because I believe a Jewish state is a terrible idea. Or because in a blog post

I said the first loyalty of the Jewish Labour Movement 'is not to their party but to a foreign country: Israel.' Which offends against example 6 in the IHRA definition. But owing prime loyalty to the Jewish state is built into Zionist ideology. That is why Jews like Edwin Montagu feared Zionism and opposed the Balfour Declaration.

So, yes, I live in a permanent state of being offended. But I'm not trying to silence anyone.

The QC Hugh Tomlinson examined the IHRA definition, found it 'unclear and confusing' and said it 'should be used with caution.' He points out:

> Any public authority which does adopt the IHRA Definition must interpret it in a way which is consistent with its own statutory obligations, particularly its obligation not to act in a matter inconsistent with the Article 10 (of the European Convention on Human Rights) right to freedom of expression. Article 10 does not permit the prohibition or sanctioning of speech unless it can be seen as a direct or indirect call for or justification of violence, hatred or intolerance. *The fact that speech is offensive to a particular group is not, of itself, a proper ground for prohibition or sanction.* The IHRA Definition should not be adopted without careful additional guidance on these issues.
>
> Public authorities are under a positive obligation to protect freedom of speech. In the case of universities and colleges this is an express statutory obligation but Article 10 requires other public authorities to take steps to ensure that everyone is permitted to participate in public debates, *even if their opinions and ideas are offensive or irritating to the public or a section of it.*

And the former High Court judge Sir Stephen Sedley states: 'No policy can be adopted or used in defiance of the law. The Convention right of free expression, now part of our domestic law by virtue of the Human Rights Act, places both negative and positive obligations on the state which may be put at risk if the IHRA definition is unthinkingly followed.'

Unfortunately, that didn't stop my council voting unthinkingly to adopt it. But, here's a turnup for the books, along with the right of Jews to self-determination they passed an amendment which gave Palestinians rights of self-determination. How do they reconcile those two rights since one negates the other? Who knows? I doubt that they gave it a moment's thought.

I doubt that Palestinian self-determination would be satisfied with a fragmented mini-state on the 22 percent of Palestine left after Israel's expansionary War of Independence. So a reasonable interpretation of the amendment would be that they voted for a Palestinian state in the whole of pre-Israel Palestine and the return of five million Palestinian refugees.

Let's put it another way: a single secular state with equal rights for all regardless of religion or ethnic origin.

Perhaps Einstein would have voted for that.

9

Theodor Herzl: Visionary or Antisemite?

Theodor Herzl is everywhere in Israel. It would be difficult to find a town without a street named after him. He is memorialised in the names of boulevards, parks, squares, a city (Herzliya), a forest, at least one restaurant, a museum, and even a national cemetery—Mount Herzl. His portrait hangs in the plenum hall of the Knesset. His birthday is observed as a national holiday, Herzl Day. This is to be expected. After all, was he not the founder of the Zionist project and the Jewish state?

What, though, does the average Israeli citizen know about Herzl? Not a lot, I suspect. Do they know he was reprimanded by his rabbi in Vienna for celebrating Christmas with a Christmas tree? Do they know he refused to have his son, Hans, circumcised? That his first solution to 'the Jewish problem' was a mass conversion of Austrian Jews to Catholicism? 'It should be done on a Sunday, in St. Stephen's Cathedral, in the middle of the day, with music and pride, publicly,' he wrote.

There's an amusing interview in which a journalist presents a number of Israeli students with a quote from Herzl and asks who they thought wrote it. Every one of them says Hitler. They are shocked to discover the truth; the Herzl they'd learned about in school could not have written such an antisemitic statement. This is the quote: 'An excellent idea enters my mind—to attract outright anti-semites and make them destroyers of Jewish wealth.'

The journalist and peace activist Uri Avnery referred to Herzl's writings as having, in places, 'a strongly antisemitic odour.' Indeed they do. Try this, for example (describing the attendees at a Berlin soirée in 1885): 'Some thirty or forty ugly little Jews and Jewesses. No consoling sight.' Clearly Herzl didn't like Jews much.

So what is going on here?

Herzl was born in Budapest in 1860. His parents were secular, assimilated, German-speaking Jews and he himself admired German culture, philosophy, art, and literature as the acme of Western civilisation. As a student at Vienna University, he joined the German nationalist fraternity Albia, whose motto was Honour, Freedom, Fatherland, though he did later resign in protest at the antisemitism that he encountered. Like many educated, German-speaking Jews, he had nothing but contempt for the mass of religious, Torah-abiding, Yiddish-speaking, shtetl-dwelling Eastern European Jews. There is nothing in his writings to suggest that he had any great attachment to Judaism or much interest in or knowledge of Judaic teaching.

And this was his dilemma. He was educated, cultured, rational, an admirer of Germany's enlightened civilisation, a model citizen of the Austro-Hungarian Empire in all respects except one: he was a Jew, the 'other.' And even though his Jewishness meant little to him, he could not divest himself of this label and so could not be fully accepted. No wonder he found the idea of converting to Christianity so appealing. 'I give praise to every Jewish parent that decides to convert to Christianity,' he wrote. And again: 'I have a son and would sooner convert today to Christianity than tomorrow so that he would start being Christian as soon as possible to spare him the injuries and discrimination that I suffered.'

His son, Hans, who wasn't circumcised at birth, seems to have had an identity crisis for most of his life. He did have himself circumcised when he was thirteen, after his father's death. In 1925, he became a Baptist, then, shortly after that, declared himself a Catholic. A year or so later, he wrote in a letter to the *London Jewish Daily Bulletin*, 'I consider myself a member of the House of Israel.' In 1930, when he was thirty-nine, he shot himself.

Ultimately, Herzl decided that conversion could not be the answer and that, as he wrote in his diary, it was empty and futile to try to combat antisemitism. In his book *Der Judenstaat*, published in 1896, he explains why: 'The Jewish question exists wherever Jews live in perceptible numbers. Where [antisemitism] does not exist, it is carried by Jews in the course of their migration. We naturally move to those places where we are not persecuted and there our presence produces persecution.... The unfortunate Jews are now carrying the seeds of Anti-Semitism into England; they have already introduced it into America.'

In a later chapter, he argues that 'the immediate cause of antisemitism is our excessive production of mediocre intellects, who cannot find an outlet downwards or upwards—that is to say, no wholesome outlet in either direction. When we sink, we become a revolutionary proletariat, the subordinate officers of all revolutionary parties; and at the same time, when we rise, there rises also our terrible power of the purse.'

In short, the responsibility for antisemitism lies with the Jews. They carry its seeds within them. It's their fault for being Jews. Herzl believed that the Jews who did not choose to live in his Judenstaat would eventually assimilate and disappear, which for him would be a good outcome. In his view, Jews were a contaminated race. 'At some dark moment in our history,' he wrote, 'some inferior human material got into our unfortunate people and blended with it.' It is no surprise then that antisemites were fans of Herzl's project.

After the First Zionist Congress in 1897, the Kaiser wrote, 'I am all in favour of the kikes going to Palestine. The sooner they take off the better.'

Der Judenstaat translates as 'The Jewish State' but it might more accurately be translated as 'The State of the Jews' because there is almost nothing that is specifically Jewish about Herzl's vision. Much of the book is concerned with the practical arrangements for transferring Jews to the Jewish state—those who remain behind, he argues, will soon disappear altogether—and for setting up the structures (physical, legal, and constitutional) of the new state. He envisages a state that more or less replicates the advanced class-based capitalist societies of Europe. 'I think a democratic monarchy and an aristocratic republic are the finest forms of a state but the Jewish state will be an improvement because we shall learn from the historic mistakes of others ... for we are a modern nation and wish to be the most modern in the world.'

And where will this state be? He hovers between Argentina—fertile land, plenty of space, sparse population, mild climate—and Palestine, 'our ever-memorable historic home.' In Palestine, he writes, 'we should there form a portion of a rampart of Europe against Asia, an outpost of civilisation as opposed to barbarism.' Zionism has always sold its state as an oasis of Western civilisation in a desert of Arab backwardness—'a villa in the jungle,' as Ehud Barak put it. Or a state that would further Britain's imperial interests in a region of great strategic importance, as Chaim Weizmann promised Balfour. Or, as one might put it now, America's post–Six-Day War watchdog in the Middle East.

Did Herzl know Palestine was already populated? Of course he did. In 1895, he wrote in his diary: 'We shall try to spirit the penniless population across the border by procuring employment for it in the transit countries, while denying it employment in our country. But the process of expropriation and the removal of the poor must be carried out discreetly and circumspectly.' Like many early Zionists, he thought that the views of the Palestinian population could be discounted and that they had no political rights and should have no say in the matter.

When he discusses the language of the new state, he dismisses Hebrew as impractical. As for Yiddish: 'We shall give up using those miserable stunted jargons, those Ghetto languages which we still employ, for these were the stealthy tongues of prisoners.' Instead, 'every man can preserve the language in which his thoughts are at home.' There will be a 'federation of tongues' until the most useful language wins out. The Jewish religion? In its place and no further. 'We shall keep our priests within the confines of their temples.... They must not interfere in the administration of the state.' There is no mention of the Sabbath or of celebrating the Jewish festivals. Even the flag has no Jewish symbolism, no Magen David, only seven golden stars on a white background.

Herzl claimed that he was motivated to argue for a Jewish state in order to solve the problem of antisemitism. But his solution was tantamount to removing the Jewish people from the world's stage, depositing them in Palestine, and erasing as far as possible any expression of Jewishness.

In 1902, Herzl published a novel called *Altneuland* (Old Newland). It is set in Palestine, where a new Jewish state has been established. He describes this new state as absorbing all the best ideals of every nation. There is no conflict with the indigenous Arab population. One of the heroes is an Arab engineer, Rashid Bey, who says: 'The Jews have made us prosperous, why should we be angry with them? We live with them as brothers, why should we not love them?' A Palace of Peace is built in Jerusalem to arbitrate in international disputes. Religion is respected but plays absolutely no part in public affairs. Many languages are spoken, and Hebrew is not the main one. Non-Jews have equal rights. A fanatical rabbi named Geyer (in German, 'geyer' is a bird that eats carrion) forms a party which attempts to disenfranchise non-Jews because 'this is a Jewish state and only Jews should have the right to citizenship.' In the end, they are defeated by the liberal opposition who argue, 'It would be immoral to exclude anyone, whatever his origin, his descent or his religion from participating in our achievements.... Our motto must be now and ever—Man you are my brother.'

Wishful thinking, maybe, but Herzl's utopian fantasy is infinitely preferable to the dystopia that is Israel today. It was, though, heavily criticised for imagining a Jewish state that had nothing Jewish about it. Ahad Ha'am (Asher Ginsberg), the writer and founder of cultural Zionism who opposed Herzl's political Zionism, denounced the book: 'Anyone examining this book will find that in their state the Jews have neither renewed nor added anything of their own. Only what they saw fragmented among the enlightened nations of Europe and America, they imitated and put together in their new land.' He also attacked Herzl's naiveté in portraying the Arab population as welcoming enthusiastically the Jewish colonists.

So the 1895 Herzl, who, in order to bring about his Jewish state, advocated removing the Arab peasants from their land so that they could be replaced by Jews, seven years later imagined a Jewish state where the relationship between Jew and Arab was harmonious and conflict-free and all were equal citizens. Doesn't this point to the impossible contradiction at the heart of the Zionist project? The state that Herzl most admired, his model state, was a European liberal democracy like Germany. In order to create that model in the state of the Jews, he had to remove from it anything that was exclusively Jewish. The less Jewish, the more democratic. The more Jewish, the more it would exclude non-Jews and therefore the less democratic it would be.

The Zionist parties that fought for and in 1948 succeeded in creating a state were Jewish nationalists. Their state would be not only of the Jews but also for the Jews: the nation-state of the Jewish people—all of them. They were clear that the state could only survive in that form by, as Herzl had explained, driving out the majority of the non-Jews who lived there. Maximum land, minimum Arabs was the political imperative.

They were with Herzl also in his contempt for Jewish life in the diaspora and were determined to create the new pioneering Jew: Hebrew-speaking, self-confident, healthy, sturdy, everything that they believed the diaspora Jew was not. 'Chazak ve-ematz,' they said: be strong and courageous. Israel would represent, as Uri Avnery put it, 'the total repudiation of all forms of Jewish life in exile, their culture and their language, Yiddish.' From Ben-Gurion on the left to Jabotinsky on the right, they expressed a distaste bordering on shame for the 'ghetto Jew' and the 'money Jew.' David Ben-Gurion (born David Grun) said of diaspora Jews: 'They have no roots. They are rootless cosmopolitans—there can be nothing worse than that.'

For Ben-Gurion, as for Herzl and Jabotinsky, the ideal Jew was 'the new Jew' (who is, it seems, always a man), preferably a 'tzabar,' born and bred in the Jewish state, the 'chalutz,' the pioneer, Hebrew-speaking, strong, healthy, outdoor, self-confident, scorning 'the sin of weakness,' everything that the diaspora Jew was not. He didn't think much of the 'Hitler Zionists,' the German Jews who had been allowed to emigrate to Palestine in the 1930s, because they came as refugees, not pioneers. He referred to Holocaust survivors and Mizrahi Jews as 'human debris.'

According to Ze'ev (formerly Vladimir) Jabotinsky:

Our starting point is to take the typical Yid of today and to imagine his diametrical opposite.... Because the Yid is ugly, sickly, and lacks decorum, we shall endow the ideal image of the Hebrew with masculine beauty. The Yid is trodden upon and easily frightened and, therefore, the Hebrew ought to be proud and independent. The Yid is despised by all and, therefore, the Hebrew ought to charm all. The Yid has accepted submission and, therefore, the Hebrew ought to learn how to command. The Yid wants to conceal his identity from strangers and, therefore, the Hebrew should look the world straight in the eye and declare: 'I am a Hebrew!'

In Israel's early years, it was possible to believe that it was a democratic state. Of course, you would have to ignore the fact that the Palestinian minority who had not fled or been driven out in the 1947–48 war were living under military rule, subject to curfews, administrative detentions, expulsions, and land theft. When I was in Israel in 1958–59, no one mentioned the word 'Palestinians.' As 'Arabs' they had no presence in public life. And the secular Israelis I mixed with were not greatly concerned about Jewishness. They considered themselves Israeli first and Jewish a long way after, if at all. For them Jewishness was the religion and its repressive laws which they resented. No politician ever called for Israel to be recognised as a Jewish state. It wasn't necessary.

But when military rule was lifted in 1966, Palestinians began to play more of a part in public life. They began to organise themselves politically. And then there was the Six-Day War and the occupation and the settler movement, and over the decades the number of Palestinians in Israel grew and they started to protest against land expropriations and house demolitions so that they began to be viewed as a problem and then as a demographic threat. But a demographic threat to what? To Israel as the nation-state of the Jewish people, of course. It's not that this self-definition had ever gone away but now it needed to be asserted. And with the two intifadas, anti-Arab racism grew and religious fanaticism, particularly among West Bank settlers, and the demand that Israel be recognised by the Palestinian leadership as a Jewish state became a deliberate political block on any genuine peace negotiations; and inevitably, inexorably, under governments of both Left and Right, Israel grew to be what it is now, a segregated, racist state where apartheid is enshrined in the recently enacted Nation-State Law.

Herzl, in *Altneuland*, solved the contradiction between a Jewish state–that is, the nation-state of the Jewish people— and a liberal democracy by virtually erasing its Jewishness. Israel has solved the same contradiction by erasing its democracy.

I wonder what Herzl would have made of this manifestation of his solution to antisemitism, this militarised ethnocracy, where the Rabbinate controls the laws pertaining to marriage, divorce, and burial; where fifty rabbis from the Orthodox religious establishment declare that Halachic law forbids Jews from renting or selling apartments to non-Jews; where two settler rabbis interpret the commandment 'Thou shalt not kill' as only applying to Jews killing other Jews, not to gentiles; where 30 percent of the Jewish population don't want to work with 'Arabs' and 50 percent of Israeli Jews would rather not have an 'Arab' as a neighbour; and where 56 percent of Israeli Jewish high school students believe that 'Arabs' should be barred from becoming members of the Knesset.

Not much like *Altneuland*, then. And it will get worse. Because Jews are not a nation. And if the Israeli nation continues to exclude the quarter of its population that is not Jewish, it will become more religious, more intent on Judaizing land and laws and policies, more repressive and more intolerant of dissident views until it reaches its journey's end as a fully formed fascist state.

10

Israel and the Labour Party: A Love Story

The suggestion that Israel's staunch supporters are infected with a brain disease called zionusitis is, of course, a joke. Or maybe it isn't. There has been another enactment of the absurdist farce called 'Antisemitism in the Labour Party.' A demonstration in Parliament Square organised by the (self-selected) British Board of Deputies and the Jewish Leadership Council demanded an end to the antisemitism which, so they claim, is now rife in Corbyn's Labour Party. It was attended by a number of Labour MPs plus various riffraff from other parties and the usual suspects from the Jewish Labour Movement. Following that, Jeremy Corbyn attended a seder organised by a group of young Jews called Jewdas and was pilloried for consorting with the wrong sort of Jews.

Of course, this has nothing to do with real antisemitism. The Board of Deputies has no problem with the antisemitism of Trump and the American white supremacists or the antisemites in Hungary and Poland, like Viktor Orban, since they are also firm supporters of Israel. Jewdas is attacked as unrepresentative because it is a non-Zionist group. Since Israel claims to represent all the Jews in the world, and since Netanyahu claims to speak for 'the Jewish people,' it would not be surprising if those who are angered by Israel's oppression of the Palestinians tweet or write criticism of

Israel that sometimes topples over into antisemitism. But a report by the Institute for Jewish Policy Research found that the level of antisemitism in the country and across the political parties, including the Labour Party, is low. The level of anti-Israelism, on the other hand, is significantly higher. And this is what the Zionist lobby, the Board of Deputies, the Jewish Labour Movement, and the Labour Friends of Israel are concerned about.

In any case, it's hard to feel sympathy for Labour MPs like John Mann, Louise Ellman, and Luciana Berger who complain of being abused online when they themselves and other Labour Friends of Israel are silent—or, worse, mouth Israeli propaganda in an attempt to justify Israel's deliberate policy of killing and wounding unarmed demonstrators, including children, in Gaza. As dupes of a foreign power, what do they expect? And, incidentally, the Tory government's now-infamous 2014 Immigration Act that created a 'hostile environment' for immigrants and asylum seekers and that aimed to turn teachers, landlords, employers, and doctors into narks for the government was unopposed by the Labour Party, including the three MPs mentioned above. The only Labour MPs who voted against were Corbyn, McDonnell, Diane Abbott, David Lammy, and Denis Skinner. So who are the racists here?

My question is why? Why are all these MPs so desperate to defend the criminal state of Israel? What is it about Israel that addles the brains of otherwise rational politicians? Why is there a Labour Friends of Israel? There isn't a Labour Friends of Myanmar. There was never a Labour Friends of apartheid South Africa. Why Israel? Some defenders of Israel—the Virgin Airline passengers who had a brain seizure when they read the word 'Palestinian' on the menu and the Daily Mail's Melanie Phillips who, when Independent Jewish Voices was formed, called it Jews for Genocide—are clearly bonkers. Others, like Angela Smith, the Labour MP who tweeted her disapproval of Corbyn's attendance at the Jewdas 'seber' (as she wrote it), and Joan Ryan, chair of Labour Friends of Israel, are, I suspect, rather dim and shamefully ignorant. But there are others who are intelligent, informed, politically aware, and perhaps critical of the Israeli government's policies yet still defend the state of Israel as a Jewish state. Do they know of the crimes committed in the name of Zionism, in the name of the Zionist state?

Stanley Cohen's book *States of Denial* describes a psychological condition in which a person knows yet doesn't know. 'Denial is understood as an unconscious defence mechanism for coping with guilt, anxiety and other disturbing emotions aroused by reality. The psyche blocks off information that is literally unthinkable or unbearable. The unconscious sets up a barrier which prevents a thought from reaching conscious knowledge.'

This would explain why it took so long for the abuses committed by Jimmy Savile and Harvey Weinstein to become a public scandal. Some people knew, yet somehow they didn't know because to accept the reality was unthinkable. Perhaps most of us live in a state of denial because otherwise life would be unbearable. We know, for example, that the threat to the planet from global warming is real, yet most of us live as if we don't know.

Cohen's book includes a quotation from Orwell, writing on nationalism, that is particularly apt when applied to Israel and Jewish nationalism: 'The nationalist not only does not disapprove of atrocities committed by his own side but he has a remarkable capacity for not even hearing about them.... In nationalist thought there are facts which are both true and untrue, known and unknown. A known fact may be so unbearable that it is habitually pushed aside and not allowed to enter into logical processes or on the other hand it may enter into every calculation and yet never be admitted as a fact, even in one's own mind.'

In the case of Israel's supporters, this brain disorder of knowing and not knowing is paralleled by the disconnect between the image of Israel as it presents itself—as it has always presented itself—to the outside world and the living reality of Israel as it is, as it has always been. For Zionists in the Jewish Labour Movement to allow the reality to reach conscious knowledge would indeed be unbearable, would strike at the core of their identity. After all, the United Synagogue proclaims 'the centrality of Israel in Jewish life.' That then becomes an absolute bar to acknowledging the reality of Israel and its history.

'The question of identity,' James Baldwin wrote, 'is a question involving the most profound panic. Identity would seem to be the garment with which one covers the nakedness of the self.'

Look at it this way. Israel was founded on ethnic cleansing, the total destruction of some four hundred Palestinian villages and on deliberate massacres of the indigenous population. Deir Yassin was the most infamous but more gruesome was the massacre at Al Dawayima on 29 October 1948 when, according to a report received by the Israeli daily *Al Ha-Mishmar*, soldiers from the 89th Battalion entered the village and killed eighty to one hundred Arab men, women, and children. 'The children they killed by breaking their heads with sticks. There was not a house without dead.... One commander ordered a sapper to put two old women in a certain house ... and to blow up the house with them. The sapper refused. The commander then ordered his men to put in the old women and the evil deed was done.... One woman, with a newborn baby in her arms, was employed to clean the courtyard where the soldiers ate. She worked a day or two. In the end they shot her and her baby.'

The report was never published. In another village, Safsaf, a report submitted to the Mapam Political Committee listed the crimes committed by Israeli soldiers: '52 men tied with a rope and dropped into a well and shot. 10 were killed. Women pleaded for mercy. Three cases of rape ... a girl aged 14 was raped. Another was killed.'

Of course, terrible things happen in war. Soldiers on all sides commit atrocities. But the point here is that the actions of the Israeli army were driven by the political imperative of establishing a Jewish state with 'maximum territory, minimum Arabs.' The blame lies not so much with the individual soldiers as with Zionist ideology. As Ben-Gurion wrote in his diary: 'Soldier eyewitnesses to these events concluded that cultured officers had turned into base murderers and this not in the heat of battle ... but out of a system of expulsion and destruction. The less Arabs remained—the better. This principle is the political motor for the expulsions and the atrocities.'

In April 1948, Tochnit Dalet, Plan D, was put into operation, giving the green light for the indigenous population to be expelled outside the borders of the state. Mass expulsions followed. In July, seventy thousand Palestinians were driven out of Lydda and Ramleh with nothing to eat or drink on an order signed by Yitzhak Rabin and approved by Ben-Gurion. It was known as the Death March. Hundreds died.

'There is nothing more moral from the viewpoint of universal human ethics than the emptying of the Jewish state of the Arabs and their transfer elsewhere,' said Mapai politician Avraham Katznelson. 'This requires the use of force.'

In December 1948, Israeli ministers discussed the atrocities. The agricultural minister, Aharon Zisling, said, 'This is something that determines the character of the nation.... Jews too have committed Nazi acts.' Finally it was decided that, in order to preserve Israel's image, nothing should be admitted.

In the same month, the UN General Assembly passed Resolution 194 which supported the right of Palestinian refugees to return to their homes. In response, Mapai, Israel's ruling party, passed the Absentee Property Law which forbade Palestinian 'infiltrators' from returning on pain of death and legalised the seizing of property belonging to those who had been expelled so that it could be given to Jews.

'It is well-known that we are the best socialists in the world ... even as we plunder the Arabs,' said Mapai politician Pinchas Lavon. So Israel was, as Shlomo Ben-Ami, Barak's foreign minister, acknowledged, 'born in sin' and stained with blood. Yet, in its own eyes and in the approving eyes of most of the non-Arab world, it was an immaculate birth in the wake of a terrible tragedy.

Prominent Labour Party politicians, both on the right, like Richard Crossman and Herbert Morrison, and on the left, like Michael Foot, Harold Laski, Aneurin Bevan, and Anthony Wedgwood Benn (before he became Tony Benn and a fierce critic of Israel), were enthusiastic supporters of the new state. Ernest Bevin, for his own political reasons, was a notable exception. After the catastrophe of the Holocaust this is perhaps not surprising. Nevertheless, it required a deliberate denial of the injustice done to the Palestinians. The massacres were ignored, or the knowledge of them was repressed. It would be decades before Israeli revisionist historians like Benny Morris, Ilan Pappé, and Avi Shlaim shed light on the real history of the Nakba. As for the mass expulsions, Israel invented a plausible explanation: the Palestinians fled because the Arab leaders told them to. There was never any evidence for this but Israel has never required any evidence for its propaganda myths. Also overlooked was the fact that, while the 1947 Partition Plan gave Israel 55 percent of Palestine (although Jews formed only 30 percent of the population and owned only 7 percent of the land) by the end of the fighting, Israel's borders had expanded to take in 78 percent of the land. Acquiring territory by war is a violation of international law but this, too, was overlooked.

The Labour Party's close relationship with and support of Zionism goes back well before the establishment of the state. It endorsed the Balfour Declaration in 1917. In 1920, Paole Zion, the British section of the International Labour Zionist Organisation (the forerunner of the Jewish Labour Movement), affiliated with the British Labour Party. In the following decades, the Labour Party supported Zionism's creeping colonisation of Palestine, the process of buying land from absentee landlords and evicting the native farmers who worked the land, a process which had begun towards the end of the nineteenth century.

Arthur Rappin, head of the Jewish National Fund in 1920, was clear about it: 'Land is the most necessary thing for establishing our roots in Palestine. Since there are hardly any more arable unsettled lands in Palestine, we are bound in each case of the purchase of land to remove the peasants who cultivate the land.'

In 1944, the Labour Party conference passed a resolution promoting free immigration of Jews into Palestine and transfer of the Arab population. 'Let the Arabs be encouraged to … move out as the Jews move in.'

Even anticolonial socialists like Michael Foot could not bring themselves to acknowledge that Zionism itself was a colonising project and that Israel was a settler state. With their racist mind-set they saw Israel as an oasis of Western civilisation in a desert of Arab backwardness. They felt an affinity with the ruling party's professed socialism, ignoring the fact that this Jewish socialism excluded the Palestinian minority, most of whom were living under military rule until 1966. They fell for the guff about 'making the desert bloom like a rose' and admired the egalitarian ideology of the kibbutzim, not realising—or unwilling to believe—that many kibbutzim were built on the ruins of Palestinian villages, that Palestinians were barred from joining and that the policy of the kibbutz movement was not to use 'Arab' labour. In supporting the Histadrut, Israel's trades union, they somehow failed to notice that it was a racist organisation dedicated to excluding Arabs from the workforce, thus following Herzl's injunction to 'spirit the penniless population across the border by denying them employment.'

The Labour Party's love affair with Israel continued despite Suez in 1956; Israel's role in the plot against Egypt escaped blame when Bevan launched his famous attack on the Tory government at the Trafalgar Square demonstration. The love affair continued despite the 1967 Six-Day War initiated by Israel's attack on Egypt; the Israeli propaganda machine went into overdrive here with a claim that Egypt had attacked Israel, a lie repeated at the UN two weeks later by Abba Eban. It continued despite Israel's occupation of the West Bank and Gaza and annexation of East Jerusalem, despite its wars against Lebanon in 1978 and 1982, despite Sabra and Shatila, and despite Israel's violent response to the first nonviolent intifada (Rabin's order to 'break their bones' was carried out to the letter by Israeli soldiers). It continued despite the settlement expansion during and after the Oslo talks, despite the wars on Gaza, despite the war on Lebanon, the siege of Gaza, the use of torture and imprisonment without trial, the Wall, the demolition of houses, the theft of water, the uprooting of olive trees, the apartheid, the everyday violations of international law, the incarceration of Palestinian children. And still they love Israel, though it should surely be clear to any rational person what sort of state Israel is.

A state unlike any other and a law unto itself. It is an anachronism: a settler state in the twenty-first century. It is, as far as I know, the only state with borders that are flexible, as they must be if Zionism's dream of a Greater Israel embracing world Jewry is to be fulfilled. The international consensus is that pre-1967 Israel defines its final borders. Israeli maps, however, have not shown the Green Line as the border of Israel since 1971, when Golda Meir declared that

Israel's borders are determined by where Jews live, not by a line on the map. It is the only state I know of that defines nationality by (supposed) ethnicity, so there is no such thing as Israeli nationality because it is a state not for its citizens but for all the Jews in the world. It is nuclear-armed, has one of the most powerful armies in the world, with the most sophisticated weaponry and has launched five aggressive wars against its neighbours yet claims always to be the victim. It uses the Holocaust to justify its oppressive policies but has treated its Holocaust survivors abysmally.

And it is a psychotic state, a state in denial. Its first myth was 'A land without a people for a people without a land' thus disappearing the indigenous people. In 1969, Golda Meir was still insisting, 'There were no such thing as Palestinians.... They did not exist.' It is a state that rewrites its own history and will not acknowledge, nor will the majority of its Jewish citizens, the suffering it has inflicted on the Palestinian inhabitants of the country it has colonised. As Shlomo Ben-Ami has written: 'Israel, as a society, suppressed the memory of its war against the local Palestinians because it couldn't really come to terms with the fact that it expelled Arabs, committed atrocities against them, dispossessed them. This was like admitting that the noble Jewish dream of statehood was stained forever by a major injustice.' No wonder then that any commemoration of the Nakba has been made illegal.

'The Israeli political establishment inflicted on Palestinians four types of denial,' noted Palestinian diplomat Afif Safieh. 'First came the denial of our very existence. Then followed the denial of our rights. All this was accompanied by the denial of our sufferings and the denial of their moral and historical responsibility for this suffering.'

So now we have a Labour shadow foreign secretary who loves Israel. She cannot accept that the Israel she loves, 'the only democracy in the Middle East,' bears little resemblance to the actual Israel. She will not see that the increasingly repressive nature of the state, the militarisation of society, the racism, and the growing religious fanaticism are the inevitable consequences of its self-definition as a Jewish state, a state that excludes its non-Jewish minority from full citizenship. She criticises the policies of the present government and believes—or professes to believe—that a change of government would remove the settlements and bring about a two-state solution. This delusion is necessary because it would be too awful to acknowledge that Israel's oppression of the Palestinians is inherent in the nature of the Zionist state and not due to this or that government's policies.

The Labour Party itself, up to and including Corbyn, is in a state of denial. It hangs its hopes on a two-state solution brought about by peace talks. There are no peace talks. There never were any genuine peace talks. The peace talks were in reality an excuse for Israel to solidify its settlement project. There is no two-state solution. The two-state solution is dead, even Jonathan Freedland can see that. But this hard reality must be denied because the alternative—a single secular state with equal rights for all (i.e., the end of the Jewish state)—is too awful to contemplate.

Is it? Really?

11

My Life as a Songwriter (or How I Failed to Become Rich and Famous) in Twenty-Three Episodes

1 The war is vivid in my memory.

I am five years old. It is the early years of the war, before the blitz. I have been evacuated with my two older sisters to Bridgewater in Somerset. I remember always feeling cold, so it must have been the winter months of early 1940. We all sleep in the same room and I hear my sisters complaining about the nasty woman who is supposed to be looking after us. Her food, they say, is awful. One day the nasty woman asks me if I would like to go to church with her on Sunday. I don't want to go but I'm a little afraid of her. She says if I go with her I will see Mickey Mouse. I would like to see Mickey Mouse. My sisters tell me she is not telling the truth. But when Sunday comes, I go with her anyway. She takes me by the hand to the church.

These are the lifelong lessons I learned from going to church: that grown-ups tell lies and that Jesus Christ is not Mickey Mouse.

Soon after that, our mother came to rescue us and take us home.

2 It is a year later, maybe more. We are being bombed. I am running down Dartmouth Park Avenue with my mother to the tube station in Tufnell Park. The wailing sirens are warning us that the Nazi bombers are coming. I don't remember why my father and my sisters aren't with us. My mother is short and stout and can't really run. But she is running. I worry that she may fall.

This memory is awakened every time I see film of people fleeing war.

3 I am thirteen at an all-boys grammar school. My parents tell me that they have enrolled me for music and piano lessons every Saturday morning at the Royal Academy of Music. I am aghast. I explain to them that I have been picked for the school under-fourteen football team that plays on Saturday mornings. They are unmoved. It's the Royal Academy of Music. I should be grateful. Football? So you're going to be a footballer when you grow up? I plead with them. In vain. The disappointment rankles for years after. 'I could have played up front for the England team, but I never even got a trial.'

4 In Hebrew, our Hashomer Hatzair leaders tell us, a hike is *tiyul*. So we are going on a *tiyul* into the countryside, me and the other teenagers in this self-styled Socialist Zionist youth movement. At midday we stop for lunch in a wooded area. One of the boys takes out a knife and starts to carve a Magen David on a tree. A leader tells him to stop. It will upset the people who live round here. 'Good,' the boy replies. 'Maybe it will start a pogrom and all the Jews will have to go to Israel.'

I carry this memory as a puzzle in my mind until I realise that Zionism and antisemitism are bosom pals.

5 I have no idea when it was. Sometime in the 1950s, surely, when I was still at school, perhaps. An all-Irish cast in a performance of Sean O'Casey's *The Plough and the Stars* in a pub theatre. Somewhere near Ladbroke Grove, was it? The details are unimportant. What remains in my memory is the impact, like a punch in the guts which made me cry out in pain and laughter. I loved the plays of O'Casey, even the later, supposedly inferior ones, like *Red Roses for Me*, the story of a strike for an extra shilling a week. 'Maybe he saw the shilling in the shape of a new world.' I've never forgotten that line.

6 November 1956. It has been a momentous year. The Soviet invasion of Hungary, the British-French-Israel invasion of Suez, Khrushchev's speech attacking Stalin, and the first performance of John Osborne's *Look Back in Anger* at the Royal Court Theatre. My ideas and convictions are now being shaken and stirred. I am in the vast crowd overflowing Trafalgar Square for the great anti-Suez demonstration. Aneurin Bevan delivers an excoriating attack on the government and particularly on the prime minister, Anthony Eden. I have never heard words used so powerfully and with such a galvanising effect on the assembled thousands. Bevan is the standard bearer for socialism in the Labour Party.

Less than a year later, Bevan, the standard bearer for socialism in the Labour Party, delivers another speech, this time to the Labour Party Conference, attacking—ridiculing—a motion calling for Britain to unilaterally abandon its nuclear weapons. It will, he says, send any foreign secretary 'naked into the conference chamber.' My trust in politicians is dust in the wind.

7 After leaving university in 1956 with no job in mind and no prospect of one, I find myself, a year later, happy to be playing the accordion in a play at the Oxford Playhouse called *The Hamlet of Stepney Green*. I don't actually think much of the play, but that's not something you must ever say or even think when embarking on a new production. I love the ambience of the theatre and the camaraderie of the actors. They give each other presents before the opening night. I believe I received a pair of socks. The director is Frank Hauser who has a habit of addressing me as 'boychik' though I'm not sure he's even Jewish. Once he reprimands me for coming late to a rehearsal. I don't mind. It makes me feel important.

8 Easter 1958. The first Aldermaston march. In the photo I am playing the accordion, not the most sensible instrument to be taking on a long walk. There is music, music all the way. The London Youth Choir is singing. Jazz bands are playing. Skiffle groups are skiffling. This is heartening. Groundbreaking. I feel hopeful.

9 June 1958. I am on the ship bringing me and a whole crowd of others—Yiddish-speaking immigrants from Eastern Europe on the middle deck, North African immigrants with babies and bundles on the lower deck, young Zionists from Western Europe on the top deck—to Israel. As Haifa comes into view, the young Zionists start singing Israeli songs and dancing the hora with dedicated enthusiasm. As we draw nearer to the port, some of them stand proudly erect and sing 'Hatikvah.' I am standing at the ship's rail next to a young Israeli, a Sabra, born in Israel, returning from a holiday in Europe. He spits into the sea-foam. 'Ach!' he grunts. 'How I hate these displays of emotion.'

10 The *ulpan* in Tel Aviv is where new immigrants go to learn Hebrew. We are a mixed gathering of Jews from Europe and the Americas. One of the Americans, Claudio, is a bank robber who broke out of a Manhattan jail after serving six years of his sentence and fled to Israel where, because he is a Jew, he has an instant right to become an Israeli citizen. The class includes some very attractive young women. One in particular catches my eye. Her face is expressive, changeable. She is actually the best student in the class. She tells me that she is working as a nurse and is from Aleppo and then Beirut. She was first assigned to a low-grade overcrowded *ulpan* for immigrants from the Arab countries until, French-speaking, she redefined herself as from Paris so she could join this superior *ulpan*. Which was fortunate because that's how we met, and that's how we later came to be married.

11 In the early 1960s, a songwriting revival is under way. Many of the songs, including some of mine, have been sparked off by the CND Aldermaston marches and the civil disobedience campaign of the Committee of a Hundred. I can't remember when or why I decided that what the movement needed was a hit West End CND musical. I finished writing it in 1963. It was about a mass disobedience campaign during a nationwide civil defence exercise. A cast of thousands. I took it to an agency in Great Newport Street run by a chain-smoking Dickensian character called Mrs. Jolly who specialised in typing playscripts. When I went to pick up the typed script, she told me she thought my musical was wonderful and that she had contacts with Foster's Theatrical Agency in Piccadilly Circus and would be happy to send it there and surely they would want to stage it.

I threw the rejection letter away. I can't remember exactly what it said, but it was pretty conclusive. Who would want to go and see something as dreary as a musical about politics? Something like that. One of the songs in it, 'Across the Hills,' lived on through the decades. And we still have our nuclear weapons.

12 One lady member of the staff clasped her head and exclaimed: 'My God! How unprofessional can you get?' Or so asserted a reviewer. My crime? To have asked the audience to fill the empty seats at the front. Not the done thing in the Wigmore Hall, an early-Edwardian, elegantly decorated, marble-walled, somewhat staid six-hundred-seater concert hall specialising in small-scale classical music concerts. It is a prestigious venue and not at all suited to the launch of an LP called *A Laugh, a Song and a Hand-Grenade*, a mix of my songs and Adrian Mitchell's poems, recorded live at Bradford and Lancaster Universities. Our contribution to the 1968 uprisings. I can't imagine what the lady staff member must have said while Adrian was delivering his 'Ode on the Assassination of President Johnson.' I don't remember how the audience responded to our musical and poetic missiles, but the shock that vibrated through the hall as people at the back rose up and scrambled for the expensive seats at the front stays in my memory still.

13 It's just before Xmas 1969 and Father Xmas is being arrested. Not just one Father Xmas but half a dozen of them, dressed in their red robes and white beards, members of the Father Xmas Union, the brainchild of a bearded American, Ed Berman, who'd founded a community action group called Interaction. They are protesting outside Selfridges against the sale of war toys to children and the exploitation of children's fantasies by religious and commercial interests and they are all arrested for breaching the peace. I'm watching this bizarre bit of street theatre on television with interest since I'd written the Father Xmas Union's anthem. I have no memory of this song now but I do remember the song I wrote for the Mother Xmas Union.

> You can stuff your own turkeys, you can make your own
> mince pies
> Here's your pretty little aprons, won't you try them on for
> size?
> 'Cos we've made the last supper, and we've made the last
> bed
> Now we're going to join the Mother Xmas Union instead.

The Father Xmas Union actually applied to affiliate with the Trades Union Congress but was turned down on the bureaucratic grounds that Father Xmases were already represented by the Union of Shopworkers.

Working with Interaction was a new experience for me. I'd been given an Arts Council grant, the only time I've ever received state funding, and I had to write songs to order, to a brief and to a deadline, mostly for their children's street theatre group, the Dogg's Troupe. I can still see them, parading through the streets dressed as moon men or comic book heroes, gathering up children and involving them in plays to encourage their creativity and subversive tendencies. My job, for which I had to cut down on the verbiage, was to write songs and chants with catchy tunes that children could easily join in with. 'It's a skule rule that you've got to go to school and it's a skule rule, you mustn't play the fool in school.' It made a cheerful change from *Dead Men Never Die*.

Ed Berman also invented the Fun Art Bus with its singing bus conductor, its driver who doubled on electric piano, its bus ticket poems, its cartoon cutout decorations, its kinetic window boxes, and its upper deck entertainment—for which my contribution was a short musical called *There's No Bussiness Like Show Bussiness*. And a song which reflected the craze for building urban motorways, 'They're Going to Build a Motorway through My Back Garden.' While it was being performed, a solemn ritual was enacted. A single daffodil in a flowerpot was carefully cut down and cemented over. Subtle stuff.

One day, I promise myself, I'll write a hit musical.

14 The 1970s saw alternative theatre groups springing up everywhere—women's theatre, political theatre, gay theatre, fringe theatre, pub theatre, lunchtime theatre, student theatre. So I decided that I'd try my hand at writing plays. Why not? Song is a form of theatre and the creation of stories and characters is its stock in trade. And maybe I'd be able to write that hit musical. The drawback was that, unlike with songwriting, I was totally dependent on the judgment of others. Well, I tried. But in the end, despite the best efforts of the International Famous Agency, my achievements didn't amount to much: one play on BBC radio's *Afternoon Theatre*, one play accepted by BBC TV but never produced, four one-act plays produced in fringe theatre venues to mixed reviews, including one at the Arts Theatre in London, and two plays translated into French and staged somewhere in France. Plus an impressive assortment of rejection letters.

The play scripts, including the putative hit musical, all impeccably typed by the chain-smoking Mrs. Jolly, now lie mouldering in a dark cupboard.

15 A more rewarding theatre experience in 1973 when I'm asked to write songs for a stage production of *They Shoot Horses, Don't They?* at the Crucible Theatre in Sheffield. Derived from Horace McCoy's novel rather than from the Jane Fonda film, it's the story of a dance marathon in the Depression years, a powerful picture of a society that manipulates people by exploiting their hopes and dreams, forcing them to compete against one another for an illusory prize. Just up my street. It's a challenge I welcomed—writing songs expressing the feelings of specific characters in a dramatic context. And I felt at home working with a community of people with a common interest and a common aim.

I regret not doing more work like this.

16 Saturday 9 July, a mass picket outside the Grunwick photo processing plant in Dollis Hill, just a few tube stops down the line from where I live. Most of the workers there are Asian immigrants from East Africa. They have been ruthlessly exploited and treated appallingly by the management and the owner, George Ward, and are striking for better conditions, better pay, and the right to join a union. The strike started in 1976 and gradually gathered Trade Union support which upsurged into mass pickets by midsummer 1977. On this day, Arthur Scargill is bringing down a contingent of

Yorkshire miners 'to support the lads on the picket line' (most of the Grunwick workers are actually women).

I am in touch with Hackney Music Workshop and we decide to bring our instruments and voices and get the assembled thousands to sing. Because we believe singing on a picket line gives heart and hope to the strikers. I have vague thoughts of doing a Pete Seeger, so I am giving my banjo a rare outing. With the possibility of more police violence, I didn't want to risk my Martin guitar anyway. I can't remember what we sang. Probably the standard American sing-along songs. 'We Shall Not Be Moved.' 'We Shall Overcome.' 'Roll the Union On.' 'Which Side Are You On?' Whatever we sang, not one voice joined us. Nobody sang. They looked and listened as an audience. There may have been a scattering of applause. But no one sang. There has been no singing on the picket line. Shouting, sloganising, and speechifying but no singing.

A year later, after the TUC went to arbitration, called off the mass pickets, and then withdrew their support, the strike ended in failure.

> Well, the government ministers talked of common sense
> And the TUC sat firmly on the fence
> And they backed resolutions, and they passed round the hat
> But they couldn't do this and they couldn't do that
> And the mass pickets were a grave embarrassment
> To the chaps in the Labour government
> So let's try moderation, let's leave it to the law
> Let's give Ward a chance, let's call it a draw
> If we use the proper channels, if we learn to say please
> If we doff our caps, if we go on our knees
> They'll grant us our rights, let's give it a try …

The defeat of the Grunwick strike was a pointer to the future, when the trade unions would be disempowered and the miners' strike broken.

17 My first children's book, *Rosa's Singing Grandfather*, was published by Viking/Puffin in 1991 and was short-listed for the Carnegie Medal in that year. Subsequently my agent, Gina Pollinger, sold the stories to an American publisher, Philomel. In April 1993 I was on tour in America and while in New York paid a visit to Philomel's offices on Madison Avenue, taking with me a copy of the Puffin edition of the book to show the story editor there. She stared at the picture on the cover, as if in shock. It shows a white grandfather and a brown-skinned granddaughter with black hair tied in topknots. There's nothing in the text to indicate that the granddaughter is mixed-race but since my family includes mixed-race granddaughters, I asked for the illustrations to show that. The story editor seemed bemused, as if she couldn't believe what she was seeing. 'How can that be?' she asked.

When the Philomel edition came out, I saw on the cover the grandfather holding hands with a white-skinned, red-haired granddaughter. Of course.

18 I once took a bus all the way across America from New York to Los Angeles. I had some idea that this would be a romantic journey. Disappointingly, I found nothing at all romantic about travelling by Greyhound bus for days and nights along endlessly straight roads which, I like to think, reflect America's restless drive and energy and desire to get somewhere, stopping in identical coffee shops, passing through identical towns with their identical malls and identical gas stations that had grown up alongside the roads, or rather had been thrown up by people who were in a hurry to move on to somewhere better. Because there's always somewhere better.

In the 1980s, England under Margaret Thatcher tried to be more like America. And I took my guitar and songs to parts of North America I never imagined I'd see. In 1970, before my first visit, I was informed by the US embassy that, because of my Communist past, I was ineligible for a visa under Section 212 (a) (28) of the Immigration and Nationality Act. But they were prepared to waive my ineligibility and, what's more, I could purge myself of this political sin entirely if I engaged in anti-Communist activity for a period of five years. How kind. So I had a waiver on my passport which often meant trouble with immigration officials.

I toured Canada and the States extensively in this decade, solo or with Roy Bailey and Frankie Armstrong. Vancouver and its wonderful festival became a second home. In many parts of the States, particularly on the West Coast, the Bay Area, New York, I found sympathetic, responsive audiences. In other parts, where audiences seemed to have no idea what I was singing about, where the only news of Britain they get is the royal family, where they know nothing about the rest of the world or even where the rest of the world is, I had the feeling that I might as well have been singing in Japanese. I think of Columbus, Ohio. Little Rock, Arkansas. What was I doing in Little Rock, Arkansas? Other audiences were more enthusiastic. In a sweetly smoky club in Garberville, which happens to be the marijuana capital of California, every song was rapturously received. They laughed at absolutely everything. There's nothing better than a pleasantly stoned audience to boost your ego.

19 I don't like to remember the 1980s. Endlessly bleak. The march of the neoliberal free marketeers into the future.

> *The Jackboot Democrats are on parade*
> *The ones who're made of money and the ones who've got*
> *   it made*
> *The top brass, the upper class, the highest of the high*
> *You can watch them on the giant screen that's blocking off*
> *   the sky.*

The defeat of the miners and the closing of the pits was a bitter blow. Coal was going to be phased out eventually but the way it was done decimated the mining communities and that was deliberate. It was hard to accept. Some couldn't accept it. A conversation with someone in a folk club ended badly because I mentioned the defeat of the miners. He became angry, insisted it wasn't a defeat. 'They went back to work with their heads held high.'

20 One episode brightened my mood. In response to Peter Wright's spill-the-beans book *Spycatcher*, about the murky deeds of MI5, the Thatcher government got the Law Lords to issue an injunction which prevented the book from being published in the UK and made illegal any quotation from the book and any reference to the events described in the book. This outrageous censorship prompted the Campaign for Press and Broadcasting Freedom to ask me to encapsulate the book in a song whose illegality would show up the absurdity of the ban. This was a challenge I couldn't resist. The book, imported from Australia, was handed to me in a brown paper bag. I stayed up half the night trying to digest its somewhat turgid prose and the next day managed to roll as much of the book as possible, including a couple of direct quotations, into a song, 'Ballad of a Spycatcher.'

> *The trouble was, says Wright, that we often were misled*
> *And the Russians always seemed to be a step or two ahead*
> *For whatever MI5 knew, the Russians knew it too*
> *And when we knew they knew, they knew we knew they*
> *   knew we knew.*

It was certainly illegal. But could we provoke a prosecution? It was published in the *New Statesman*. Disappointingly, nothing happened. Then it was a single with Billy Bragg and the Oyster Band. That, too, provoked no legal response. Would the DJs play it? They were at first cautious. But gradually it got airplay. Some DJs obviously thought it was all a bit of a lark and began to plug it. Sales picked up. It got into the indie singles charts. For the first time in my life I was buying the *New Musical Express* to see how high in the charts it had risen. But wait a minute. This wasn't what was intended. This was supposed to cause political embarrassment for the government. Eventually it got to number five. So much for subversive intentions.

21 On 15 February 2003, I come out of the tube onto the Embankment and am uplifted by the sight of a vast mass of people—including children and babies—assembled there, waving banners, bearing placards, chanting slogans, flooding the street, protesting against the planned Bush-Blair war on Iraq. Surely this is the biggest demonstration I have ever taken part in: people from different political persuasions and different religious faiths, part of a worldwide protest against a war, based on a lie, that everyone knows would devastate a country and murder its people. We surge past the Houses of Parliament, confident that this is a demonstration that our democratically elected representatives cannot ignore. We the people have spoken.

22 It is Friday, 8 April 2005. We are standing on the Mount of Olives in Jerusalem looking down on the skirmishes involving Palestinian youths and Israeli soldiers and police. There is a lot of anger and tension because a group of religious settlers are threatening to invade Temple Mount and Palestinian worshippers are being stopped from entering the mosque. In the East Jerusalem cafe where we had eaten lunch, the woman proprietor had complained to us that her son, who lives on the Mount of Olives, was not being allowed to visit her. 'But they are allowing the Jews in,' she said. I would like to tell her that they are not Jews, they are Israelis, that I'm Jewish and am opposed to Israel and its policies. But this is probably not the best time to have a discussion about identity. A group of very angry Palestinian boys and men are alongside us, also watching the running battles below. One of them asks me aggressively, 'Are you Jewish?' 'We're British,' I reply, without a moment's thought.

23 The morning light leaks through the curtains as I open my eyes. Appropriately, it is Friday the thirteenth. December 2019. There was no way I was going to stay up to watch the election results. Rina has her iPad. 'Is it bad?' I ask. 'Terrible,' she says.

12

Coronavirus: March 2020

I breakfast in the kitchen where I can look out through the windows onto the back garden. Every morning, I watch the squirrels—three of them, two parents and a young one—performing their circus tricks, chasing each other, skittering along the top of the wooden fence, lightly leaping onto the garden shed, springing upwards onto the oak tree, swaying and swinging from branch to branch, then gliding down onto the shed and scampering back along the fence. Why do they do it? Natural exuberance? The joy of living? Excitement at the approach of spring? Do they know something we don't?

As Rina and I are eighty-five, we have been advised to self-isolate (a horrible expression) so the garden has taken on a new importance. It's an ordinary suburban garden, nothing special. But it's quiet, screened from traffic and the hubbub of the city. I can immerse myself in the green of the garden, and the rest of the world dissolves. The trees are just now coming into leaf. The star magnolia is a white foam of flowers. Soon the lilac will be blossoming. They say that this virus onslaught could continue for months, maybe even into next year, so we will have all the time in the world to observe the way the garden changes through the seasons.

Do you know how this thing started? Don't believe what they tell you. This is what happened. On the first stroke of midnight, as Wuhan teetered on the brink of the new year, all the animals in Wuhan's market gathered together and, under the guidance of a wise old dog called Mutt, decided to incubate a virus that would cause a complete shutdown of human society; bring the whole monstrous, mindless machine juddering to a halt so that we humans might consider our crimes and pay penance for them.

Is it working?

The government claims it is following the science but everything it does seems misguided, too little, too late. It makes a decision on one day and reverses it a few days later. The 'herd immunity' theory lasted about five minutes. It won't mass-test, and then maybe it will. On Monday it wants to stop schools and nurseries closing, and then it announces on Wednesday that all schools will close on Friday. It's the Boris Johnson U-turn dance. Johnson advises people to avoid pubs, clubs, restaurants, cafes, theatres, and cinemas but doesn't mandate closing them until the very last minute, probably too late. Why not? Could it be because if these venues are compelled to close they can claim insurance for loss of revenue, but if they close of their accord—as most have now done—they are no longer insured? Like the banks, insurance companies cannot be allowed to fail.

Of course, the government is keeping one panicky eye on the economic impact of this pandemic, balancing the measures needed to minimise the number of deaths against the damage to the economy these measures will cause. 'Many more families are going to lose their loved ones before their time,' announces Johnson, putting on his very best fake-sympathy face. He forgot to add 'unnecessarily.'

After a decade of austerity, the National Health Service, starved of funds, marketised, partly privatised (a process started by Blair and New Labour), is in no fit state to deal with this crisis. Its staff are overworked and underpaid. It is short of doctors and nurses by one hundred thousand. There aren't enough intensive care beds. There aren't enough ventilators or surgical masks. Doctors and nurses complain that their protective clothing is inadequate. They want to know why they are not being tested for the virus before they are inundated with infected patients. And—can you believe this?—the Conservative Party responsible for this dire state of affairs, the Conservative Party whose policies have plunged four million children into poverty, made millions of families dependent on food banks, and forced three hundred thousand into homelessness, has just been reelected with a massive majority.

Isn't this the very definition of insanity? The squirrels must be laughing their heads off.

Sometimes we have visitors. Not human ones, of course, as we're self-isolating. Apart from the resident robin and the blackbirds nesting in the hedge, the usual suburban garden birds come and go: pigeons, magpies, blue tits, great tits, goldfinches, and the very occasional woodpecker. And a flock of screaming parakeets, escapees from somewhere. A black cat circles the garden every day, as if to remind us that it owns at least a half-share. From time to time a fox drops in, emerges from a hole in the fence in the corner of the garden, trots around the lawn, examines whatever catches its interest, lies on the grass for a bit if it's sunny, scratches itself, yawns, then, in no hurry at all, saunters back to the fence and makes its way out. There used to be more wildlife. When we moved in about fifty-five years ago, we could hear hedgehogs copulating outside our bedroom window and an owl hooting from a neighbouring garden.

Thanks to Attlee's Labour government, the UK has a nuclear deterrent (a bomb with a bloody Union Jack on top of it, as I remember Ernest Bevin demanding) so we are well protected against invaders. With the support of the Labour Party (despite Corbyn), Parliament voted to renew the Trident nuclear missile system. As of now, this consists of four nuclear-powered submarines, each one carrying sixteen Trident missiles. There are 3 nuclear warheads on every missile, so that's 48 missiles on every submarine, 192 in all. Each warhead has eight times the power of the Hiroshima bomb. At least one submarine is on patrol at all times. How insane is that?

> *Trident, Trident, money down the drain*
> *It can kill all living creatures and then kill them all again.*

The estimated cost of renewing it is at least one hundred billion pounds. Fifteen hundred thirty-six Hiroshimas. All that power, yet it couldn't deter a tiny organism no bigger than one-millionth of an inch from entering the country, closing down society, and killing thousands.

I see that an economist has suggested in the *Guardian* that this crisis is (God help us!) 'an opportunity to do capitalism differently.' As if this monstrous, mindless, malignant machine can be humanised.

What's the betting that the Coronavirus Bill now coming before Parliament will be used to curtail our freedoms and human rights?

Time for another sanity session. Let's see what the squirrels are up to.

13

Stay-at-Home Days

Let us accept
No division between day and day
All days are equal
Let Monday walk
Side by side with Thursday
Let us abolish the chummy superiority of Saturday
And the tight-laced snootiness of Sunday
And—why not?—yes, a month of Sundays
Except that
After we have brought about
The democracy of days
We will start on the weeks
And the years until—
Time is a seamless flow
A land unmarked, unbounded
A world without cause or consequence
In which we will laze
Happy as innocence
And in a timeless daze.

14

Interview with Robb Johnson

It's August 2020, the first year of the plague, when we start this long-distance conversation. Originally we thought we might get together in person in Leon's garden, but that hasn't happened so far. So far, this dialogue has been an exchange of emails. In the past we have talked in each other's gardens, before gigs, after gigs, on the way to gigs, in cars, the very occasional aeroplane, trains—Leon was aghast when on our way to kick Trident missiles out of Faslane I returned from the buffet with a can of Stella for breakfast. 'That's the point of travelling by train,' I said, 'I get to have a beer' and also to write our only joint composition, 'Bury Trident,' which wouldn't have happened in a car. We have talked late into the night and we probably know more about each other than we might care to admit. In 1999, on the first night of our first and only European tourette together, Leon was beating me easily at chess in Leuven when my second son decided to be born five weeks early, so we never did play Europe together. In 2011, on our first and only tourette of the western coast of Canada and the United States, thanks to Leon arranging for me to borrow a Martin guitar that was as old as I was, I became a convert to Martin guitars. In 2020, I bought an old Martin D35 twelve-string on the internet. I wrote to Leon that one of the few positives about lockdown for me was that I was enjoying playing guitar again, just for the fun of it. Leon replied:

You're right, it is something pleasurable. My first guitar was a nylon-string Kessler bought in the early 1950s. It had a lovely mellow sound and I still enjoy hearing it on the Galliards recordings. I'm even tempted to get out my Harmony twelve-string from the '60s … but probably not. Too hard on the fingers. But I do remember enjoying playing it with the 3 City 4. I was playing my Kessler at the time so it was great to get a big sound on songs like 'The Hour When the Ship Comes In' and '15 Million Plastic Bags.'

I write that I think the key of C suits my voice better than the key of D I usually play and sing in. Leon responds that for him, the key of C means the song 'Freight Train.'
Elizabeth Cotten rather than Lonnie Donegan. Apparently she wrote it when she was twelve years old. I saw her at the Vancouver Festival in 1981. She was already in her late eighties. You can see her on YouTube playing the guitar left-handed and upside down, so she's picking out the tune with her thumb. I think I learned to play it, clawhammer style, from a recording by Peggy Seeger who, of course, learned it from Elizabeth Cotten. I remember—or possibly I'm invent-ing it—meeting the American guitar/banjo/mandolin player Ralph Rinzler on a train sometime in the late 1950s and telling him I'd mastered the clawhammer. As I had my nylon-string guitar with me, I showed him how I did it.

'No,' he said. 'You're using too many fingers.' I still use too many fingers.

For as long as I have known Leon, he has always only ever played the same guitar, a beautiful, slightly battered old Martin. I ask him where it came from.
In 1970 I played my first American gig at Izzy Young's Folklore Center in New York and bought my Martin guitar there. I took to it straight away—a bright tone and easy on my fingers. It changed the way I played—less classical, more folk.

Do you think of yourself as a 'folk artiste'?

Definitely not a folk artist or folksinger. I think that label is for people who sing songs from the folk tradition. As you will remember, we tried to establish 'English chanson' as an alternative to 'folksinger' or 'singer-songwriter,' but it didn't quite catch on. Although some reviews have described my songs as in the style of French chanson.

So—how did you come to spend a lifetime writing songs in a style that perhaps defies any description other than 'Rosselsong'?

My childhood in our North London flat during the war was enlivened by music and song, much of it provided by my father's fine tenor voice singing operatic arias or Neapolitan classics like 'O Sole Mio' or Yiddish folk songs. We had a wind-up gramophone on which to play our collection of 78 rpm records, including some of those Soviet songs that succeeded so well in moulding my sympathies. And, of course, absolutely essential for our entertainment, we had the wireless. The BBC Home Service and *Forces Favourites* featured a variety of songs, from the morale-boosting, like 'We'll Meet Again' and 'Roll Out the Barrel' (what was that about?), to the faintly exotic, like 'Chattanooga Choo Choo' and Bing Crosby crooning 'Where the b-b-b-blue of the night / Meets the gold of the day / Someone waits for me.' I listened and absorbed indiscriminately.

Believe it or not, I first discovered the joy of singing together in the school scouts. The memory of singing 'Ging Gang Goolie' round the campfire while the sparks ascended into the night sky lingers with me still. That we were singing gibberish in no way lessened the feeling of being elevated.

So becoming a songwriter wasn't so much a conscious decision, more the outcome of an emotional response to experience?

From my childhood into my teenage years, I seem to have followed a song trail leading almost inevitably to a place and a time when I would be writing songs.

Song, singing together, was central to my experience in the Zionist youth movement, Hashomer Hatzair. I started to understand how song could be used to bring people together, to make them feel that they were all part of the same exciting project. So we sang Israeli songs about driving southwards to Eilat, through the desert with the breeze blowing, not realising that the song celebrated Israel's theft of Palestinian land beyond what was granted in the UN Partition Plan. 'Hey Daroma.'

This is something we talk about endlessly, the role of song in political struggle. In the 1950s you were growing up in a decade when the folk revivals on both sides of the Atlantic were seen as culturally significant and politically committed.

Yes, in the early 1950s, the folk revival tiptoed into my consciousness. I bought Topic 78s, which I still have, of Ewan MacColl singing songs that gave a voice to the ones who do the work for, and are exploited by, the capitalist system, songs like 'Fourpence a Day' and 'The Wark o' the Weavers.' I started learning the guitar, went to meetings of the university folk song society (named after Saint Lawrence, for some reason), may even have tried to perform a folk song or two myself, which I soon realised was a mistake.

I joined the London Youth Choir and with them sang harmonies on peace songs, political songs, songs from around the world at political events, in streets and markets and at the World Youth Festivals on the other side of the Iron Curtain. And then I joined the great skiffle craze with a weekly session at the White Horse in Hampstead, singing Woody Guthrie's songs and other 'people's songs.' By this time, I saw song and singing as an uplifting experience, an expression of solidarity and a way of sharing stories and raising political awareness.

The idea of being a writer had always attracted me. I'd written poems for the school magazine. I'd written short stories, a few of which I still have, mouldering in a cupboard somewhere. I'd written my first song, the 'Grace Kelly Calypso,' in 1956 and accompanied it on my nylon-string Kessler guitar. That was fun, so I wrote a couple more songs which had the decency to exit my memory not long after I'd written them. But becoming a literary gent seemed a far-off aspiration.

Nonetheless, in the 1950s, 'folk music' wasn't simply about curating old songs—new writing was an important and welcome feature of the folk revival?

Yes. At the end of the 1950s, everything came nicely together for an outbreak of songwriting. As redefined by MacColl and Lloyd, folk song was a class-based music, the musical culture of the lower classes, a living tradition in which new songs challenging the status quo could and should be written. Folk clubs were springing up all over the country where young people came, angry at the way politics was being conducted, bored with the commercial music industry, eager to hear songs that reflected their lives, their aspirations, their politics. Skiffle had already broken the professionals' hold on music making. And if anyone could make music, why couldn't everyone write songs? There was plenty to write about with the revival of political action, notably the mass movement of CND. And all sorts of people—from academics like Alex Comfort to science fiction writers like John Brunner to Labour MPs like Stan Crowther to young journalists like Fred (Karl) Dallas—were expressing themselves in song.

So I took the opportunity. Expressing my view of what was happening in the world by combining words and music seemed like a wonderful idea. Inventing stories, juggling words, and finding the melody to keep them flying through the air became a task that I welcomed. Just as wonderful was the fact that, unlike in other art forms where I would have to jump through hoops in order to be accepted, I could communicate my songs directly to an audience open to hearing new songs. They were the final arbiter. That was when I started to write songs seriously (and humorously). And I carried on through the decades, learning as I went.

And you have earned your living by your songwriting wits ever since?
Until around 1974 I was part-time teaching to supplement my song/performing/writing income. Since then I've been a full-time performer/writer, but income was supplemented by my wife, Rina, who was also working until she retired in 1995. I never wrote or expected my songs to make me rich or famous, though in the 1960s I did assign some of my songs to publishers, presumably in the hope that they would in some way popularise them. Big mistake. I do think, however, that if I had had more access to the media, my songs might have reached more people.

How has your writing evolved over the decades? What have you learned about songwriting?
The first thing I learned is that there's a lot more to writing songs than throwing words at a tune.

Many of my early songs were satirical/topical like 'Stand Firm,' 'Dear John Profumo,' and 'Song of the Free Press.' I really enjoyed reading Alexander Pope's satires at school and was much impressed by his claim that he could make the objects of his satirical poetry tremble in their shoes. ('Yes, I am proud I must be proud to see / Men not afraid of God afraid of me.') I suppose I thought my satirical songs might have the same effect. Satire was all the rage at the time. I was writing satirical pieces for the socialist paper *Tribune*. And then there was the TV programme *That Was the Week That Was* (or *TW3*) which featured a few of my songs—the one about the Labour Party and one about judges ('Hey ring-a-ding-ding I love the spring when the pretty birds sing so gaily / I don my wig and dance a jig and dole out judgments daily').

I think writing that sort of song taught me a lot about the craft of songwriting: how to shape a verse and how to balance and polish lines, for instance. I began to understand that the first words that come into your head are not necessarily the best ones and that the task is to find the most effective words, not just for their meanings but also for their sound. I learned that it's better to avoid the predictable. And I learned something about using rhymes for humorous effect and also how to rhyme better.

In my early songs, I was pretty relaxed about rhyming. I thought it was near enough if I rhymed 'come' with 'fun.' Then one day I sang 'Tim McGuire' to Ned Sherrin, the producer of *TW3*. I used to go and sing my latest satirical barb to him to try to persuade him to use it on his programme. 'Tim McGuire' is in no way satirical, so I don't know what I was thinking. Anyway, he cruelly suggested that I should improve my rhyming skills. He was, of course, correct. So I decided then that if I wanted a perfect rhyme it should be a perfect rhyme, not an approximation, that if the song demanded a half rhyme, it should be a half rhyme, and that the rhyming pattern should be consistent. And that it was just laziness to avoid, rather than solve, the problems that songwriting presents.

Does all this matter? Well, to some songwriters, obviously not. It certainly mattered to Georges Brassens because you won't find a duff rhyme anywhere in his songs. Rhyme certainly mattered to W.S. Gilbert, Noel Coward, and the lyricists for the best American musicals. In Stephen Sondheim's *Finishing the Hat* there's a whole section on the importance of rhyme, which he calls 'the glue that holds the song together.' I agree that sometimes in serious songs rhymes can sound glib, obtrusive, clever maybe. Too final. Which is why I preferred half rhyme for the last couplets of the verses in 'The World Turned Upside Down.'

Form is important in songwriting, I think. It constrains the content but also gives it shape and sharpness. The tension between form and content, between what you are trying to say and the limited form in which you have to say it, is what makes song interesting.

My experience of trying to translate Brel and Piaf chansons into English makes me think that French as a language rhymes a lot more readily than English. So many words end with the same sound.
Yes, it's probably true that it's easier to rhyme in French. But Brassens' rhymings are much more complex and wide-ranging than just the past tense thing. Glancing through his songs, he doesn't seem to use that rhyme much at all. He does rhyme 'pas' with 'appas' and 'que' with 'qu'eux,' which I don't think would be acceptable in English but is, I believe, seen as a clever rhyme in French. And he sometimes rhymes the second syllable of a word with the first syllable of another word, as in 'Voici la ron- / de des jurons,' which is why I tried to do the same in my song about him.

My view is that, though he absolutely denied that he was a poet and said he wrote 'chansonettes,' he still saw his songs as a form of poetry so wanted them to look right on the page. That would explain why, unlike Brel, the voice in his songs is always that of Brassens.

It's interesting to note that you are sometimes referred to as 'the English Brassens' yet the voice in a Rosselsong is not always apparently your voice. One characteristic of Rosselsong writing is how—over the decades—your songs have developed a more complex range of voices.
I was learning with every song that I wrote and from many songs that I heard. I learned that song works better when it is focused on the particular and the visual. I learned that the 'I' in a song doesn't have to be the singer/songwriter but can be an invented character, as in 'Invisible Married Breakfast Blues.' Brel is the master of this sort of song. I saw his performance at the Albert Hall in 1966, and it was riveting.

He became the different characters his songs created. Pure theatre. And it made me see song as a form of theatre, with stories and characters at their centre.

And I also learned that there are different ways of approaching songwriting and that my way is just my way. But certainly what I learned made me a better songwriter and better able to tackle a wider range of subject matter.

Your songs have also explored the possibilities of more complex structures, playing with, pushing the limits of, but remaining recognisably within the reference points of popular song.
I soon found that the standard folk form of verse and chorus was too limiting for what I wanted to express. I'm not big on all-join-in choruses. More complex song forms—as in 'Susie' for instance—allowed for more interesting melodic forms. I learned how music in a song affects the way the lyrics are communicated; that a melody that rises has a different emotional effect from one that falls and one that leaps large intervals will add a different something from one that hovers around the same few notes; that the role of music is to support, punctuate, dramatise the lyrics. I also learned that it's sometimes a good idea to discard the guitar when looking for the melody for a song since, with the guitar, I was getting bogged down in the same chord sequences. I could never, for instance, have written the tune for 'The World's Police' from playing the guitar since the chord sequences are quite alien to me. Working from the piano gave me greater freedom.

You don't work with drums though?
Drums? Not for me. The only track of mine with drums was 'Ballad of a Spycatcher' with the Oyster Band and Billy Bragg. Since the aim was to embarrass the Thatcher government over their banning of Peter Wright's tell-all book, we needed to attract as big a popular response as possible, hence the band, drums, and Billy Bragg. But I don't sing my songs

in strict time so I felt regimented when recording it and hemmed in when performing it live. I found it really difficult to sing the lyrics in the way I wanted to when the drums were marching me onwards.

Do you have any thoughts on rhythm in songs? Time signatures?
For me, it's the lyrics that determine the time signature, that decide whether the song is in 2/4, 3/4, 6/8. They all have a different flavour. I've used less common time signatures in two songs. In 'Garden of Stone,' the lyrics dictated that the pattern of the song was alternating 3/4 verses and 7/4 verses, which was interesting. And in 'My Daughter, My Son,' I deliberately wrote the words of the agitated, anxious mother in an irregular 5/4 rhythm: *Children so tender / heedless of danger / Cars that deliver/ death while you play.*

What do you think are the top ten songs you have written?
Top ten songs? That is difficult. They tend to change as I change and my perception of them changes and the times change, and audiences change. So tomorrow there may be a different choice but as of now this is my choice in alphabetical order: 'Barney's Epic Homer,' 'Monologue,' 'My Father's Jewish World,' 'Song of the Olive Tree,' 'Stand Up for Judas,' 'Story Line,' 'Susie,' 'We Sell Everything,' 'Who Reaps the Profits? Who Pays the Price?,' 'The World Turned Upside Down,' and 'Wo Sind die Elefanten?' That's eleven. I've chosen them because they all tell stories—the best song form in my view—but also work on another level as commentaries or critiques. The language is vigorous, heightened colloquial speech with sparky images, aiming to be precise, rather than generalised, visual rather than abstract, resonant rather than flat. The form and rhyming are consistent, and, though they tend to be wordy, especially 'We Sell Everything,' there is a deliberate use of internal rhymes, alliteration, and assonance to make them easy on the tongue and the ear. The melodic

settings sustain the lyrics but also, I hope, are appealing in themselves. Their purpose is to provoke thought—and sometimes laughter—and to touch the emotions. In my estimation they mostly do that. They can, I think, be listened to many times and remain fresh and enjoyable. There are lines in these songs that I'm particularly pleased to have found— 'Now it's my father's face that meets me in the mirror'; 'We make no headlines dying by degrees'—and a triple rhyme in 'Wo Sind Die Elefanten?' that provides an almost perfect ending. Of course, they all have flaws, but they are, in my view, among the best I've been able to write.

My evaluation of the songs may not tally with the audience's, but audience response must be taken into account because songs only exist in a relationship with an audience. This particularly affects my choice of 'Song of the Olive Tree' and 'The World Turned Upside Down,' which have had a wide and enduring appeal.

What would be your top ten songs by other writers, the songs that have influenced you or that you admire? As well as your professed fondness for Brassens and Brel, I know we once talked about how we both admired Piaf's 'Les Amants d'un Jour.' I was surprised, however, when you once said you were very fond of the band Dr. Hook and the Medicine Show.

Yes, I do think 'Les Amants d'un Jour' is a great song. Perfectly formed. I suppose you could argue that the lovers are somewhat romanticised, symbolic rather than real, but it's the woman washing the glasses in this seedy hotel who is at the centre of the song. I've looked up the songwriters: Claude Delécluse and Michelle Senlis and Marguerite Monnot. So, nine more songs. Other French ones: probably Brel's 'Le Port d'Amsterdam,' the power of which kind of stunned me when I first heard it; Brassens' touching 'La Non-Demande en Mariage,' with its intricate rhymes and metaphors; Anne Sylvestre's 'Que Vous Êtes Beaux,' Aristide Bruant's 'Les

Canuts,' Dory Previn's 'Lady with a Braid,' Bob Dylan's 'A Hard Rain's a-Gonna Fall,' Brecht and Eisler's 'Song of a German Mother,' Adrian Mitchell's '15 Million Plastic Bags' (to which I put a tune), and 'Elsie,' a lovely song by Canadian singer and songwriter Marie-Lynn Hammond about her rebellious grandmother.

I enjoyed Dr. Hook largely because I like the quirky songwriting of Shel Silverstein—like 'The Cover of *Rolling Stone*.' He makes me laugh.

It's often a subjective choice and cannot always be explained in analytical terms. I could have included your songs, 'Winter Turns to Spring' or 'Be Reasonable,' and other British songwriters—Sandra Kerr, Jim Woodland, John Pole, Ewan MacColl, of course—as well as American ones, but I thought I would mainly focus on less well known songs that made an impression on me when I first heard them.

Class and poverty are elements fundamental to the narrative of 'Les Amants d'un Jour,' but it's perhaps surprising that neither of the next two writers you cite, Brel and Brassens, are generally thought of as political songwriters. Dylan's 'Hard Rain' and Brecht and Eisler's 'Song of a German Mother' are, however, clearly songs of political commitment. What are your thoughts on the question of political engagement and songwriting?

It's true that neither Brel nor Brassens wrote overtly political songs. Nothing as direct as, say, Boris Vian's 'Le Déserteur.' Brel probably wrote more songs about death than about anything specifically political. There's the unspecific anti-war 'La Colombe,' there's 'Jaurès,' and that's about it, I think.

Brassens actually addresses this question in the book I've got: *Brassens par Brassens*. He says he was, of course, against the war in Indochina. But did he have the right to tell young people not to go to the war, to desert? At the risk of being arrested, of being executed, of being rejected by their family, of being rejected years later, because they had been deserters, by the woman they wanted to marry? He maintains that it's too easy to talk of being committed (engagé): 'Mais je me suis engagé quand même.' 'Those who didn't want to go to war found reasons in my songs. They were there. Only you have to look for them because I don't express them directly. But someone who loves my songs can be incited to desert.' He says he has great sympathy for conscientious objectors but will never advise anyone to do it. It's for everyone to decide for themselves.

If he is referring to Vian's song, then it's not accurate to say that it tells anyone what to do. It tells a story, creates a character (it was not Brassens' style to do that) who is sick of wars and what they do to people and decides to refuse his call up papers. But I have some sympathy with what Brassens is saying. I think a songwriter has an obligation to engage with the world (and Brassens insists that his songs do that: 'On ne peut pas ne pas s'engager quand on écrit') but that doesn't mean he or she is obliged to write songs about every political event or songs that directly state the songwriter's opinions or tell people what to do. Brassens mocks people who think that to be 'engagé il faut que vous énonciez des faits.'

Do you think being identified as a writer of songs that overtly engage with political ideas and events engenders expectations that prove restrictive for such songwriters?
I remember being reprimanded decades ago for not writing a song about Ireland, as if a songwriter has to have an answer to every problem. Of course I had opinions, but I didn't see the point in stating the obvious and couldn't find a story to express how I viewed what I saw happening. I didn't write a song about the Vietnam War either. I have written a number of songs that tell stories about Palestine and Israel, perhaps because I am more emotionally involved in that situation.

Brassens was apparently criticised for not writing a song about the student uprising in May 1968 or about the events in

Larzac, where the government planned to extend a military base that would destroy peasant communities. He insists that he has taken a position on Larzac. You only have to listen to my songs, he argues. When you listen to my songs, it's clear which side I am on. 'Comment voulez-vous que j'écrive une chanson en disant "Laissez le Larzac aux paysans"?' (The equivalent of 'Give Ireland back to the Irish,' I suppose.)

For Brassens, that sort of protest song would be crude, inartistic, and pointless. Campaigning songs are vitally important, of course, in strengthening resolve, bolstering solidarity, creating a community of the converted. But I question whether they are interesting enough to be sung on concert platforms. Brassens did write an antiwar song, 'La Guerre de 14–18,' a satirical song that surveys history's great wars, admits their merits but decides that his favourite is 'la guerre de quatorz' dix-huit.' His style is to approach his subject matter obliquely, not directly. And it is true, as he asserts, that you know which side he is on because his view of the world emerges from the stories he tells in his songs—freethinking, anarchistic, mocking and rejecting money and power and the badges and uniforms of authority, valuing friendship, generosity, and empathy. Does a songwriter have to write overtly political songs to prove that he or she is 'engagé'?

Most art sooner or later comes up against the understanding and the expectations of whichever audience it meets with. You have been writing songs in the age of the singer-songwriter, when a significant aspect of the relationship between artist and audience is that this relationship is publicly enacted, realised through live performance. Do you enjoy the act of performance?
I never wanted to be a performer. I relished singing with others—choirs in the 1950s, a skiffle group when skiffle was all the rage, a group called Ha Nodedim (The Ramblers) with two young American women when I was in Israel in

1958–59, then the Galliards folk group, with Shirley Bland, Robin Hall and Jimmie MacGregor, in the first years of the 1960s. After that there was a group I formed called The Three City Four with Marian McKenzie, Ralph Trainer and Martin Carthy. When Martin left to go solo, Roy Bailey joined us, though fortunately for me, Martin continued to contribute his inventive guitar accompaniments to my subsequent solo recordings.

I loved being part of a group sound, especially when I was able to arrange the harmonies, as I did in the Galliards, The Three City Four and later with Roy Bailey and Frankie Armstrong. The Galliards did a lot of radio and television, concert halls, the Scottish Miners' Gala in Edinburgh (standing in for Paul Robeson) but I don't remember ever being nervous. I never imagined the attention was focused on me.

When I started singing my own songs solo in folk clubs in the 1960s, that all changed. All eyes were now on me. I developed nerves. I had to start thinking about how to present myself, how to relate to the audience. Should I talk to the audience? That's not something I'd ever had to do before. What would I wear? My first thought was that I should be just the same on stage as I was off. No showbiz flourishes for me. I'd wear the same casual, everyday clothes I wore at home or in the cinema. That would be the authentic me. But, of course, that doesn't work. Even the decision to wear my everyday casual clothes for a performance turns them into a uniform. In the end, I decided the performance me would always wear a red shirt and black trousers. Red and black. Anarchist colours.

I know Piaf also soon favoured an unostentatious, everyday black dress—the sort of serviceable clothing a woman might wear working in a bar, washing glasses in a cheap hotel. Brel favoured an anonymous dark suit, white shirt, and dark tie that would become increasingly rumpled throughout the evening of his energetic performances of his dramatic songs. Neither of them bothered with long introductions to their songs. Piaf occasionally name-checked writers, but in the United States she sometimes felt the need to explain a song to audiences—in heavily accented English. But generally they seemed to expect audiences would pay attention and keep up. I have the impression that generally English-language audiences, particularly folk audiences, like it when their hands are being held by singers who gently give them proper introductions to songs so they know what to expect.

When I saw Brassens on stage, I was struck by the fact that he never addressed the audience, never said a word to them, never introduced his songs. That wouldn't do for me. I needed to talk to the audience to feel comfortable on stage. Introducing songs is also something I had to learn. My preferred venue was one where I could see the audience and make easy contact. On the other hand, I don't feel comfortable talking about my songs. I feel they should speak for themselves. Ideally, I thought, the introductions should be crafted to be part of the performance rather than an interruption to the song flow. Difficult to achieve, but I started early on using quotations, newspaper cuttings, bits of poems, anything to link the songs while avoiding the obvious.

You were also one of the first songwriters to develop the idea of a concept performance, a fixed, structured sequence of songs and introductions?

Yes, eventually the quotations and the newspaper cuttings led to a number of scripted shows: *My Life as a Songwriter (or How I Failed to Become Rich and Famous)*; *Life Is What You Make It*, launched at the Edinburgh Festival with Roy Bailey and a couple of actors; the shows I did with Roy and Frankie Armstrong—the antinuclear *No Cause for Alarm* and *Love, Loneliness and Laundry* and one about the Spanish Civil War; one I did with socialist magician Ian Saville called *Look at It This Way*; and *The Greatest Drummer in the World*, a children's show based on a story I'd written. And, of course, the one you and I did together about Tom Paine: *The Liberty Tree*. In a way, performing these shows gave me the most satisfaction and compensated for the fact that I had failed to become a playwright.

You said you started off playing in folk clubs, and you like situations where you can see the audience. How do you feel about performing on bigger stages?
It took me a long time to get used to performing in large concert venues. I remember the first time I sang solo at the Albert Hall in 1966, a concert headlined by Buffy Sainte-Marie, called *The New Songs*. I was terrified. The lights were dazzling. My brain was frozen. My hands and fingers were out of control. I couldn't see anyone. I was trying to communicate across a vast and empty space which swallowed up the audience and left me isolated. I had no way of gauging the audience reaction. I didn't enjoy it, though it got me a kind review in the Tory *Daily Telegraph*.

I'm more used to large venues, concert halls, and festival stages now but I still get nervous. I think my songs work better in more intimate spaces where nothing distracts from the words.

Is there a particular or typical Rosselsong audience, do you think?
I sing for any audience willing to listen. I know many of my songs make demands on an audience's concentration and some people aren't used to that. There's an assumption that those who come to hear me sing share, to some degree, my politics, but I like to think that even if they don't, the songs are open enough to allow them in. I've had negative reactions to some of my songs—'Stand Up for Judas,' for example, 'On Her Silver Jubilee,' and particularly my songs on Palestine and Israel. And that's fine. I'm not trying to please everybody or make the audience love me.

Your performance style presents as being very direct, characterised by honesty rather than artifice. You said earlier you rejected 'showbiz' flourishes but even wearing your everyday clothes on stage you felt there was an inevitable difference between 'performance me' and the 'authentic me.' Do you value authenticity over artifice?

I think all art is artifice. As Magritte noted, 'Ceci n'est pas une pipe.' A play in the theatre is not real life but an invented and constructed representation of reality. The people in a play are not real people. They're actors playing roles and expressing emotions and views that they may not, as non-actors, even feel or believe. As Julian Barnes pointed out, all fiction is a lie. That story never happened; those characters never existed. But it is, or should be, a lie in the service of the truth. So it's an authentic reaching for a truth about the way we live, expressed through a deceit or stratagem.

Song is no different. Even the most one-dimensional song form, seemingly the most authentic—songwriters expressing directly their views on the state of the world or the state of their love life—involves verbal, formal, melodic choices which distinguish it from real speech. But I think that's not a very creative use of the song form. In my view, the more artifice, the more invention, the more layered, the more alive, the more interesting the song will be.

What is an authentic song? Maybe a song that needs to be—has to be—written. The urge to write it is overwhelming. By that definition, there are a lot of inauthentic songs around. They may be beautifully formed and expressed, but they lack conviction. There is no vital spark.

So is that a Rosselsong characteristic? Have your songs always been animated by that vital spark of conviction?

Way back when I was discovering how to write songs, I wrote a song called 'Men.' I didn't have to write it. There was no inner compulsion. But a cabaret performer who'd started singing a few of my satirical songs asked if I'd write a song for a friend of his, a woman who worked in cabaret. I think she had performed at the Windmill Theatre, its dying days as it turned out. So I did. I tried to write it well, to make it funny, to express what I imagined she might identify with. ('I've seen the whole assortment from the dashing to the drab / From the gentlemen who ask you to the macho men who grab.') It was an interesting exercise. That's all it was—a songwriting exercise. And I got paid for it. Around the same time, I wrote a song called 'The Bachelor's Complaint.' Even the title was a lie because I was already married by that time. I used to sing it when I was with the Galliards. Audiences found it funny. They laughed, a pleasing response for a song-writer. It was also undoubtedly sexist. It really didn't have to be written. It nearly made an appearance on the opening night of the satirical TV show *That Was the Week That Was*, to be sung by a cabaret performer, Lance Percival. Fortunately, for whatever reason, the producer cut it at the last minute. I was there and remember being deeply disappointed. It was a hit show. I could have had a lucrative career writing inau-thentic songs for cabaret.

On the whole, I'm in favour of honesty in songwrit-ing. But I also think there's room for pleasurable songs that are smart and well composed, even if they don't have the conviction of authenticity. The songwriting scene would be somewhat bare without them.

Your performances and your songs are very personal but not confes-sional. Autobiographical elements are generally, I think, digested and processed whenever they appear in a Rosselsong. And used sparingly.
Yes, I think that's right. Personal experience in itself is not necessarily interesting. It becomes interesting when it reso-nates with a broader experience—makes a political point, if you like. As the feminist slogan has it, the personal is political. And the other way round. The political is personal.

But your father is an obvious presence, identified as a protagonist, almost, in some of your songs—'The Song of the Old Communist,' 'My Father's Jewish World.'

Well, I think those two songs exemplify what I'm trying to say. 'Song of the Old Communist' is not specifically about my father, though his beliefs play a part in it. The protagonist is a fictional character representing what any loyal Communist Party member must have felt keeping the faith during those years of hope, struggle, and sometimes despair. The biographical details in 'My Father's Jewish World' are accurate but it's more than my father's story—it's about trying to find a positive Jewish identity.

Your father was a working musician, I think. I notice that hearing his 'fine tenor voice singing operatic arias' is where your account of your interest in song begins.

I owe my life to opera. Literally. This is the story. Sometime in the early 1920s, two young working-class Jewish women, Debbie and Mary, refugees from the tsarist empire who live in Whitechapel, are queuing outside a theatre to buy the cheapest gallery seats for the Carl Rosa Company's performance of an opera, the name of which has slipped my mind. Let's say it's *The Pearl Fishers*. A young man who is carrying a parcel is also intent on seeing the opera up in the gods. He too is a Jewish refugee from tsarist Russia, having arrived in England in 1914. He sees the women and thinks that if he can engage them in conversation he'll be able to jump the queue. And he is rather attracted to the one named Mary. She asks him what he is carrying. He says it's the score of the opera so he can check the way the singers are performing the arias. He tells her he is studying singing and intends to be an opera singer. They don't have much of a formal education, nor do they have much money but they're willing to spend the little that they have watching and listening to a musical form supposedly reserved for the elite because they are in love with opera and soon after with each other. My parents met at the opera. Lucky for me.

Is your Jewish heritage a significant factor in your understanding of the relationship between the personal and the political?
I think the belief, inculcated at an early age, that Jews should always be on the side of the oppressed played a part in forming my political outlook. Also, being Jewish, even secular Jewish, means that you never quite belong, you are, as my song says, looking at the world from the outside and so may be more sceptical of received truths, patriotisms, and nationalisms. That's why Zionism, which is Jewish nationalism, seems like a negation of the values of diaspora Judaism.

So 'Leon Rosselson' appears in Rosselsongs—mediated and fabricated by the process of creativity anyway—primarily as a social identity rather than as an individual biography?
Maybe more as a fictional character.

Is the absence of 'individual' biography in your work the result of individual modesty or aesthetic preference?
Both.

What was your reaction to the 2019 election?
I was devastated. I expected it to be bad but not that bad. The last chance of a progressive, socialist government destroyed by the secret state, the security services, the media (I've cancelled my subscription to the *Guardian*), the right-wing Labour MPs, and the Zionist lobby. I'm going to die under a Tory government. Doubtless we were naïve in believing that 'they' would ever permit a socialist and a campaigner for Palestinian rights to become prime minister. The almost-success of Corbyn in the 2017 election gave them a shock. After that it was war. But how did we ever let them get away with the fake antisemitism smear campaign? How come the

Zionist Jewish Labour Movement wasn't expelled for putting loyalty to a foreign state before loyalty to the Labour Party? For them, for the Board of Deputies, for the Labour Friends of Israel MPs, for the wretched Chief Rabbi, a man who joined a racist settler demonstration in Jerusalem where 'Death to Arabs' was the slogan of choice, nothing matters more than the so-called Jewish state. They would far rather have a government led by Boris Johnson, a serial liar, a racist, sexist, incompetent bluffer, and, judging by his novel where Jews are portrayed as controlling the media, an antisemite, because he is a staunch friend of Israel. And if that results in greater inequality, more families on the bread line, more children going hungry, more austerity, pay restraint, privatisation of public services, more environmentally damaging projects like HS2 [high-speed railway]. Collateral damage in the service of Israel. Sometimes I think the Zionists' love affair with Israel is a form of insanity. Of course, Corbyn didn't help by conceding to his enemies, abandoning his allies, and accepting the IHRA definition of antisemitism.

And now those who subverted the Corbyn project are in charge of the Labour Party. Their leader is 'a Zionist without qualification' which means he is the creature of a foreign power. A hollow man presiding over a shadow cabinet of nonentities. He has no personality and no belief in anything except witch-hunting the left, anti-Zionists, and all who support justice for Palestinians out of the Labour Party. He can't even hold to account this devious, mendacious, corrupt government's mishandling of the pandemic. Her Majesty's very loyal opposition. The establishment can breathe a sigh of relief. This is the Labour Party they love.

So what do we do now?

Good question. What's your answer?
I think it's the job of a songwriter to ask questions, not provide answers. What do we do now? I'm sure resistance

to the depredations and injustices of capitalism will continue despite governments like ours trying to criminalise protests (ten years for toppling a statue). But I doubt in the few years I've got left I'll see any radical change.

— • —

It must be nearly ten years now since Leon first announced he was giving up writing songs. He never quite managed it, of course, and there was the 2016 album Where Are the Barricades?— *Rosselsongs asking awkward questions, with Leon's characteristic balance of wit and anger, tenderness and intelligence.*

His body of work, the integrity of his creative voice, the consistent quality of his song-mongering, and his record of creative partnerships, are absolutely unrivalled by any of his contemporaries. He is truly the colossus of English songwriting.

One final anecdote; I am sure everybody who's known or worked with him would have their favourite Leon story, and this is possibly mine.

We got asked to play a solidarity benefit (i.e., we weren't getting paid) in this squatted church hall in Hackney. The vicar next door was perfectly happy his hall was being put to good use as a cultural centre for Hackney's lively, colourful, and inclusive anarchist community. Indeed, the anarchist doing the programming of cultural events was a little bit like a vicar running the traditional church youth club for local delinquents, only instead of offering the local alienated youth recreational opportunities like chess and table tennis, he was determined to broaden the cultural horizons of the local anarchos by booking Leon and me for a Friday night instead of the usual customary standard-issue noisy punk band the anarchos favoured.

Leon drives us, and we arrive at the church hall much earlier than the suggested time of 10:00 p.m. It's a long drive across London from Wembley to Hackney, so we're hoping we might start early and so head back before midnight.

The squat is empty, apart from the indefatigably chilled and positive organiser, who explains that the gig won't start until at least 11:00 p.m. because the anarchos would all be in the pub till then. There is also a video art installation to fire up at some point too. Time ticks slowly by. A few non-anarchos turn up to see Leon. Could we start at 10:30 perhaps, we suggest? Eventually it's democratically decided that the video thing should start up at 10:30. I am happy to play first, as the masses start arriving once the pub shuts, so on I go at about five to eleven. Sure enough, after about ten minutes, the revolution turns up in twos and threes, then fours and fives, and soon there's an avalanche of sixes and sevens, already seriously pissed and armed with takeaway tinnies to see off any chance of the unwelcome return of sobriety before the proper onset of alcoholic oblivion arrives in due course. They more or less ignore me after a few amiable, puzzled stares (what, no drums and overdriven guitars? weird), and their cheery, beery camaraderie soon drowns out the PA. Leon's first set is similarly amiably ignored; Leon has already explained in this interview, 'I'm not trying to please everybody or make the audience love me,' which is, of course, pretty much your perfect total punk rock manifesto. So Leon plays what he wants, but, of course, in these circumstances 'The Neighbour's Cat' doesn't stand the proverbial cat's chance in hell, let alone in a squatted church hall in Hackney after the pubs shut on a Friday night, so Leon gives up after about four songs and says I should have another bash if I wanted, then we could go home.

I duly bash away at some of my more bashable songs, but even these don't necessarily attract anything more than a few passing, momentarily curious glances. Meanwhile the few non-anarchos who have come to see Leon are a bit miffed that they have come to see Leon, actually paid the voluntary suggested solidarity entry donation that no one else has, and not actually heard him. So Leon kindly agrees to have another go. The organiser takes the microphone and loudly reintroduces Leon and loudly suggests that if people would just reduce their conversation level from bellowing to exuberant, then other people would be able to enjoy, or at least hear, the performance. The anarchos, being generally at the amiable and good-willed stage of inebriation, nod and carry on talking not quite as loudly as before. Leon grits his teeth and returns to the mike, but after a couple of songs the exuberance of the audience is clearly winning. Leon does another song—even I'm not sure what it is—and thanks them for having us and all but inaudibly announces 'This will be the last song.' He strums an E chord on the venerable Martin and sings 'In 1649 to Saint George's Hill—' and the whole hall full of totally pissed-sideways anarchos shuts the fuck up instantly, stands to attention, sticks its collective clenched fist proudly in the air, and sings along, word for word.

Radical change or what?

Index

"Passim" (literally "scattered") indicates intermittent discussion of a topic over a cluster of pages.

accordion, 16, 121, 122
'Across the Hills' (Rosselson), 19
Ahad Ha'am, 105
Albert Hall, 154; Brel concert, 68, 145
Ali, Tariq, 32, 43
'All Along the Watchtower' (Dylan), 61
Almanac Singers, 46, 76, 77
Altneuland (Herzl), 104–5, 108
'Les Amants d'un Jour,' 148
Anti-Capitalist Roadshow, 46
anthems: CND march, 17; Father Xmas Union, 124; labour, 56–57; World Youth Festivals, 11, 14–15
antinuclear movement, 16–18, 21, 50, 77, 123, 138
antisemitism, 81–86 passim, 100–102 passim, 109–10, 120, 158; IHRA definition, 92–99 passim
Arendt, Hannah, 94, 95
Armitage, Simon, 59
Armstrong, Frankie, 45, 129, 152, 153
Armstrong, Tommy, 56
Attlee, Clement, 5, 22, 135
Avnery, Uri, 101

'The Bachelor's Complaint' (Rosselson), 156
Bahro, Rudolf, 43
Bailey, Roy, 45, 87, 129, 152, 153
Baldwin, James, 112
Balfour Declaration, 94, 98, 115
'Ballad of a Spycatcher' (Rosselson), 21–22, 130–31, 146
'Ballad of Rivka and Mohammed' (Rosselson), 95
banjo, 58, 64, 127
Barak, Ehud, 103
Beersheva, 64–65
Ben-Ami, Shlomo, 117
Ben-Gurion, David, 106
Benn, Tony, 53
Berlin: Herzl, 101; Israeli emigres, 69
Berlin Wall: fall of, 44–45, 47
Berman, Ed, 124, 125
Bevan, Aneurin, 12, 116, 121
Bevin, Ernest, 6, 114, 135
Bible. Gospels, 81–89
Biermann, Wolf, 43–44
Black Dwarf, 30, 32
Blair, Tony, 22, 37, 41–43, 131, 134
Bolshevik Revolution. *See* Russian Revolution
Bragg, Billy, 57, 130, 146

Brassens, Georges, 64–71 passim, 145, 149–53 passim; 'La Guerre de 14–18,' 67, 151; 'La Non-Demande en Mariage,' 68, 148

Brecht, Bertolt, 60, 74, 76; 'Song of a German Mother,' 149

Brel, Jacques, 68–69, 70, 71, 145–46, 152; 'Le Port d'Amsterdam,' 148

'Bringing the News from Nowhere' (Rosselson), 36–37

Bruant, Aristide: 'Les Canuts,' 148–49

Brunner, John: 'H Bombs Thunder,' 17

'Bury Trident' (Rosselson), 138

Bush, Alan, 34

Cameron, David, 80

Campaign for Nuclear Disarmament (CND), 16–18, 21, 50, 77, 123

campfire singing, 140

Cardew, Cornelius, 78

Carson, Rachel: *Silent Spring*, 24

Carthy, Martin, 152

censorship, 130, 146

Chicago: events of 1968, 28; Joe Hill funeral, 54; Rosselson family, 10

children, Palestinian, 95–96, 110, 112–13, 116, 131–32

children's books, 4, 128

China, 34

Christ. *See* Jesus Christ

Christianity: Herzl and son, 101–2

clawhammer-style guitar playing, 139

CND. *See* Campaign for Nuclear Disarmament (CND)

coal miners, 56, 130

Cohen, Leonard, 62–63

Cohen, Stanley: *States of Denial*, 111

Cohn-Bendit, Daniel, 31

Cold War, 5, 6, 11, 16. *See also* 'Ballad of a Spycatcher' (Rosselson)

Colston, Edward: Bristol statue toppling, 51

Committee of a Hundred, 123

Communist Party of Czechoslovakia. *See* Czech Communist Party

Communist Party of Great Britain (CPGB), 2, 10, 18, 20, 32, 33, 46, 157; folk songs and, 75, 77

Communist Party USA, 75, 76

Connell, Jim: 'Red Flag,' 56, 57, 58

Conservative Party (UK), 37, 51, 158; Cameron, 80; elections of 2019, 132, 135; Jam and, 80; Thatcher, 36, 37, 46, 128, 130, 146

Corbyn, Jeremy, 50, 58, 109, 158, 159

Cotten, Elizabeth, 139

COVID-19 pandemic, 133–37 passim

Cuba, 35

Cuban Missile Crisis, 18

Cuban Revolution, 16, 19–20, 35

Czech Communist Party, 33

Daily Worker (UK), 2, 5, 12, 13, 20

Dallas, Karl: 'Djugashvili,' 46

demonstrations: CND and Aldermaston marches, 16–18 passim, 77, 122, 123; France, 1968, 31–33 passim; Grosvenor Square, 29; Grunwick strike, 126–27; Iraq War, 38, 131; singing, 16–17, 54; Trafalgar Square, 12, 18, 116, 121

denial, 111; inflicted on Palestinians, 114, 117; Labour Party, 118

'Le Déserteur' (Vian), 149

The Divided Self (Laing), 24

'Djugashvili' (Dallas), 46

Dogg's Troupe, 125

'Don't Get Married, Girls'
  (Rosselson), 44
drama. *See* plays
dress for performance. *See*
  performance dress
Dr. Hook and the Medicine Show,
  148, 149
drums, 146
Dubcek, Alexander, 33
Dylan, Bob, 59–62, 63; 'All Along
  the Watchtower' (Dylan), 61;
  'Hard Rain's a-Gonna Fall,' 60,
  149

Eastern Europe: Soviet Bloc. *See*
  Soviet Bloc
East Germany, 43, 44
Eden, Anthony, 12, 121
Einstein, Albert, 94
Eisler, Hanns, 75; 'Song of a
  German Mother,' 149
'Eton Rifles' (Weller), 80

Father Xmas Union, 124
Feffer, Itzik, 20
Ferré, Leo, 70, 71
Flavius Josephus. *See* Josephus,
  Flavius
'Flower Power = Bread'
  (Rosselson), 23
Folklore Center, New York City,
  139
Foot, Michael, 115
France, 59, 150–51; 'La
  Carmagnole,' 55; events
  of 1968, 30–33, 150; singer-
  songwriters, 64–73, 145–53
  passim
Free German Youth, 43
French language, 66–67;
  rhyming, 145
Fryer, Peter, 12

Gaitskell, Hugh, 22
Galliards, 20, 139, 152, 156
Garberville, California, 129

'Garden of Stone' (Rosselson), 147
Gardner, Carl, ed.: *Media, Politics
  and Culture*, 77
Gaza, 93, 95, 110, 116
Gellhorn, Martha, 29
'General Lockjaw Reviews the
  Troops' (Rosselson), 39
Germany, 43–44; Herzl, 101, 105;
  Israeli emigres, 69; Nazis,
  74, 96, 97; Weimar Republic,
  75–76
Ginsberg, Allen, 25, 26
Ginsberg, Asher. *See* Ahad Ha'am
Goldman, Emma, 24, 26
Goodman, Paul, 24, 25
Gorbachev, Mikhail, 44, 45
Gospels (New Testament). *See*
  Bible. Gospels
grammar school, 5, 120
'La Guerre de 14–18' (Brassens),
  67, 151
Guevara, Che, 19, 34, 35
guitar models, 127, 138–39, 142
Guthrie, Woody, 76, 141

Hackney Music Workshop, 58,
  127
Hackney squat performance,
  160–62
Hammond, Marie-Lynn: 'Elsie,'
  149
Ha Nodedim, 64, 151
Ha Ofarim, 69
Harrison, Paul, 87
Hashomer Hatzair, 120, 141
Hasted, John: 'It Was When We
  Went to Moscow,' 11
Hauser, Frank, 121
'H Bombs Thunder' (Brunner), 17
Hebrew, 96, 104, 106, 122
Heiman, Joha, 68
Hellman, Leon, 64
Henry Cow, 78
Herodians, 84
Herzl, Hans, 101–2

Herzl, Theodor, 100–108; *Altneuland*, 104–5, 108; *Der Judenstaat*, 102, 103
Histadrut, 116
Hitler, Adolf, 74, 76, 100
Hoffman, Abbie, 26, 28

immigration policy, 110, 129
Independent Jewish Voices, 110
Industrial Workers of the World (IWW), 53–56 passim
Interaction (group), 124–25
International Holocaust Remembrance Alliance (IHRA), 92–99 passim, 159
International Marxist Group, 30
interracial families in children's books. *See* mixed-race families in children's books
Iraq War, 38, 39, 131
Israel, 50, 63–69 passim, 91–118 passim, 122, 131–32, 151–52; songs, 141, 154
'It Was When We Went to Moscow' (Hasted), 11

Jabotinsky, Ze'ev, 106–7
Jackson, Mahalia, 64, 65–66
Jam (band), 80
Jesus Christ, 81–89
Jewdas, 109, 111
Jewish Labour Movement, 97–98, 109–15 passim, 159
Jews and Jewishness, 5, 50, 81–89 passim, 120, 131–32, 157–58; Soviet emigres, 10. *See also* 'My Father's Jewish World' (Rosselson); Zionism
Johnson, Boris, 134, 159; 2019 election, 132, 158
Johnson, Robb, 45, 47; Rosselson interview, 138–62
Jones, Mary Harris: 'Mother,' 54
Josephus, Flavius, 83–86 passim
Judas Iscariot, 82–89 passim
Der Judenstaat (Herzl), 102, 103

Judt, Tony, 22

Katznelson, Avraham, 113
Khrushchev, Nikita, 9–19 passim, 121
Knut, Betty, 66, 71

Labour Friends of Israel, 110, 111, 159
Labour Party (UK), 20–22 passim, 37, 39, 50–51, 53, 158–59; 'antisemitism' and, 95, 96–97, 109; Attlee, 5, 22, 135; Blair, 22, 37, 41–43, 131, 134; Corbyn, 50, 58, 109, 158, 159; Gaitskell, 22; Israel and, 109–18 passim. *See also* Red Wedge
labour songs, 53–58 passim
Laing, R.D., 25; *Divided Self*, 24
Latin America, 34; New Song, 58. *See also* Cuba
A Laugh, a Song and a Hand-Grenade (Mitchell and Rosselson), 29, 123–24
Lemisch, Jesse, 77, 79, 80
Lloyd, A.L., 77
London Youth Choir, 10, 34, 122, 141
Lydda Death March, 65, 113

Maccoby, Hyam: *Revolution in Judaea*, 83
MacColl, Ewan, 46, 77, 141, 149
Machover, Moshe, 94, 97
Manchester University: 'antisemitism' and, 95–96
'The Man That Waters the Workers' Beer,' 58
Maoists, 34, 78
Marcuse, Herbert, 25; *One-Dimensional Man*, 24
Martin guitars, 127, 138, 139
Marx, Karl, 4, 8, 25, 26
The Mayor of MacDougal Street (Van Ronk), 60–61

Media, Politics and Culture: A Socialist View (Gardner), 77
Meir, Golda, 116–17
'Men' (Rosselson), 155–56
misogyny, 68–69
Mitchell, Adrian: *A Laugh, a Song and a Hand-Grenade*, 29, 123–24
mixed-race families in children's books, 128
Montagu, Edwin, 94, 98
Morning Star, 13, 26, 34
Morris, William, 56; *News from Nowhere*, 36
Moscow, 8–9; Robeson, 20; State Yiddish Theatre, 20; World Youth Festival, 1957, 14–16
Mother Xmas Union, 124
musicals, 123, 125, 144
Music for Socialism, 77–78
'My Daughter, My Son' (Rosselson), 71, 147
'My Father's Jewish World' (Rosselson), 147, 157
My Song Is My Own, 57

National Health Service (NHS), 22, 37, 134
nationalism: Orwell on, 111
'The Neighborhood Bully' (Dylan), 63
News from Nowhere (Morris), 36
New York City, 69, 128, 139
Nobel Prize for Literature: Dylan, 59–60
'La Non-Demande en Mariage' (Brassens), 68, 148
nuclear arms, 135–36. *See also* antinuclear movement

'Old Man Atom' (Partlow), 6
One-Dimensional Man (Marcuse), 24
'On Her Silver Jubilee' (Rosselson), 154
opera, 157–58
Orwell, George, 111

Owen, Wilfred, 63

Palestinians, 65, 90–99 passim, 103–18 passim, 131–32, 141, 154, 159; Lydda Death March, 65, 113; massacres, 112. *See also* children, Palestinian
Paole Zion, 115
Pappé, Ilan, 94, 114
Paris: Brassens, 67; events of 1968, 30–33
Partlow, Vern: 'Old Man Atom,' 6
People's Liberation Music (PLM), 78
Percival, Lance, 156
performance dress, 152
Pharisees, 82, 84–85, 86
Piaf, Edith, 145, 148, 152–53
Pilate, Pontius, 84
plays, 120–22, 125–26, 154. *See also* musicals
poetry-song distinction. *See* song-poetry distinction
Poland, 12, 45; Prague Spring, 33
Political Song Network, 45–46
Pollinger, Gina, 128
Pollitt, Harry, 2
'Postcards from Cuba' (Rosselson), 35
Previn, Dory: 'Lady with a Braid,' 149
protests. *See* demonstrations
publishers: children's books, 128; music, 143

Rabin, Yitzhak, 113, 116
radio, 2, 87, 126, 140, 152
Ramle, 65
Rappin, Arthur, 115
Red and Green Song Magazine, 47
Red and Green Umbrella Club, 45, 46
Red Balune, 78
'The Red Flag' (Connell), 56, 57, 58
Redskins (band), 80
Red Wedge, 78

Reece, Florence: 'Which Side Are You On?', 54, 56, 127
Regev, Mark, 96
Reichstadt, Etty and Avraham, 69
Revolution in Judaea: Jesus and the Jewish Resistance (Maccoby), 83
Ricks, Christopher, 61
Rinzler, Ralph, 139
Robeson, Paul, 20–21, 152
Rock Against Racism, 78, 79
Roman occupation of Judaea, Galilee, and Samaria, 81–88 passim
Rosa's Singing Grandfather (Rosselson), 128
Rosen, Mike, 46
Rosselson, Rina, 122–23, 132, 133, 143
Roundhouse, London, 25
Roy, Arundhati, 51
Rubin, Jerry, 26, 28
'The Rules of the Game' (Rosselson), 29–30
Russian Revolution, 13

Sadducees, 84–85
Safieh, Afif, 117
Sainte-Marie, Buffy, 154
Samuel, Ralph, 46
satire, 143, 144, 155–56; in chanson, 67, 151
Saville, Ian, 153
Scouts (UK), 140
Sedley, Stephen, 67, 98–99
Seeger, Peggy, 139
Seeger, Pete, 44, 76, 127
Sherrin, Ned, 144
Sherwood, Marika, 95
'She Was Crazy, He Was Mad' (Rosselson), 24
Silent Spring (Carson), 24
Silverstein, Shel, 149
Sing, 10–11, 17
skiffle, 122, 141, 142, 151; in 'Talking Moscow Blues,' 15
Smith, Angela, 110–11
Socialist Workers Party, 30, 74, 80

'So Long, Marianne' (Cohen), 62
Sondheim, Stephen, 62, 144
'Song for the Trico Women Workers,' 57
'Song of the Old Communist' (Rosselson), 14, 157
'Song of the Olive Tree' (Rosselson), 147, 148
song-poetry distinction, 59–63
Songs for City Squares (Rosselson), 64
Songs for Socialists, 56
Soviet Bloc, 33, 34, 45; collapse, 44–45
Soviet Union, 1–21 passim, 30, 34, 44–45, 51, 121; in 'Ballad of a Spycatcher' (Rosselson), 130; Hungary invasion, 12, 121; songs, 140; World War II, 1–3, 76
Spycatcher: The Candid Autobiography of a Senior Intelligence Officer (Wright), 130, 146
Stalin, Joseph, 3, 8, 9, 12, 20, 75, 121
Stalinism, 9, 46
'Stand Firm' (Rosselson), 18, 143
'Stand Up for Judas' (Rosselson), 81, 86–89 passim, 147, 154
Starmer, Keir, 51
States of Denial (Cohen), 111
street theatre, 124–25
strikes, 54–58 passim, 76; in children's books, 4; coal miners (UK), 127, 130; France (1968), 31, 32; Grunwick, 126–27; in plays, 121; Zealots, 85
'Sus Etz,' 69
'Susie' (Rosselson), 146, 147
'Suzanne' (Cohen), 62–63
Sylvestre, Anne, 68, 70, 71; 'Que Vous Êtes Beaux,' 148

'Talking Moscow Blues' (Rosselson), 15
television, 143, 144, 156
Thackray, Jake, 70

Thatcher, Margaret, 36, 37, 46, 128, 130, 146
That Was the Week That Was (TW3), 143, 144, 156
theatre. *See* plays; street theatre
They Shoot Horses, Don't They? (stage production), 126
Thornberry, Emily (Labour shadow foreign secretary), 117–18
Three City Four, 152
time signatures, 147
Tomlinson, Hugh, 98
'Topside Down Party' (Rosselson), 27
Torah, 85
Trades Union Congress (TUC), 124, 127
train travel, 138
Trotsky, Leon, 30, 75

unions, 53–58 passim, 124, 126–27
United Nations: Committee on the Rights of the Child, 96; Palestinian right to return, 113–14
United States: Communist Party, 75, 76; folksingers, 44, 60–61, 76, 127, 139; pop music, 140; singer-songwriters, 59–63 passim, 76; Rosselson family, 10; Rosselson first gig in, 139; transcontinental bus trip, 128–29; visa denial and passport waiver, 128–29. *See also* Chicago; New York City; Vietnam War; Yippies

Vaizey, Ed, 80
Van Ronk, Dave: *Mayor of MacDougal Street*, 60–61
Vian, Boris, 71; 'Le Déserteur,' 149, 150
Vietnam War, 21, 23, 27–29 passim, 58, 150
Virgin Atlantic, 90, 110

Vonnegut, Kurt, Jr., 69–70

Warsaw, 12, 33
Weller, Paul: 'Eton Rifles,' 80
'We Sell Everything' (Rosselson), 147
'We Shall Overcome,' 44, 54, 127
West Germany, 43
'Where Are the Barricades?' (Rosselson), 39
Where Are the Barricades (Rosselson), 160
'Where Are the Elephants?' (Rosselson). *See* 'Wo Sind die Elefanten?' (Rosselson)
'Which Side Are You On?' (Reece), 54, 56, 127
Widgery, David, 74–75, 79
Willis, Norman, 58
Wilson, Harold, 21–22
wireless. *See* radio
Wobblies. *See* Industrial Workers of the World (IWW)
Woodland, Jim, 45, 149
'The World Turned Upside Down' (Rosselson), 52, 144, 147, 148, 162
World War II, 1–3, 76, 119–20
World Youth Festivals, 11–12, 141; Moscow (1957), 11, 14–16
'Wo Sind die Elefanten?' (Rosselson), 44, 47–49, 147, 148
Wright, Peter: *Spycatcher*, 130, 146

Yiddish, 2, 7, 93, 101, 104, 106, 122, 140
Yippies, 26–28
Yosef ben Matityahu. *See* Josephus, Flavius
Young Communist League (YCL), 10, 12

Zappa, Frank, 79
Zionism, 63, 66, 90–99 passim, 120, 158
Zisling, Aharon, 113

About the Authors

Leon Rosselson has been at the forefront of songwriting in England for over sixty years. He started his performing career in the early days of the folk revival as a member of the Galliards with whom he made many radio and TV broadcasts and concert appearances. He began writing songs seriously (and humorously) in the early 1960s and has yet to stop. His early songs were topical-satirical, but he broadened out from there, absorbing different influences. He has performed at every conceivable venue around the UK and has toured worldwide. He has recorded many albums and published two songbooks. His song 'The World Turned Upside Down' was taken into the pop charts by Billy Bragg and covered by artists including Dick Gaughan and Chumbawamba. Leon has also had seventeen children's books published, the first of which, *Rosa's Singing Grandfather*, was shortlisted for the Carnegie Medal in 1991.

Robb Johnson worked as a classroom teacher by day and a songwriter by night beginning in 1980. Among his many releases is the 5-CD career-retrospective collection *A Reasonable History of Impossible Demands*. He is also the author of *The People's Republic of Neverland: The Child versus the State*, based on his experiences as a teacher.

ABOUT PM PRESS

PM Press is an independent, radical publisher
of books and media to educate, entertain, and
inspire. Founded in 2007 by a small group of
people with decades of publishing, media, and
organizing experience, PM Press amplifies the
voices of radical authors, artists, and activists.
Our aim is to deliver bold political ideas and vital stories to all walks
of life and arm the dreamers to demand the impossible. We have sold
millions of copies of our books, most often one at a time, face to face.
We're old enough to know what we're doing and young enough to know
what's at stake. Join us to create a better world.

PM Press
PO Box 23912
Oakland, CA 94623
www.pmpress.org

PM Press in Europe
europe@pmpress.org
www.pmpress.org.uk

FRIENDS OF PM PRESS

These are indisputably momentous times—the financial system is melting down globally and the Empire is stumbling. Now more than ever there is a vital need for radical ideas.

In the many years since its founding—and on a mere shoestring—PM Press has risen to the formidable challenge of publishing and distributing knowledge and entertainment for the struggles ahead. With hundreds of releases to date, we have published an impressive and stimulating array of literature, art, music, politics, and culture. Using every available medium, we've succeeded in connecting those hungry for ideas and information to those putting them into practice.

Friends of PM allows you to directly help impact, amplify, and revitalize the discourse and actions of radical writers, filmmakers, and artists. It provides us with a stable foundation from which we can build upon our early successes and provides a much-needed subsidy for the materials that can't necessarily pay their own way. You can help make that happen—and receive every new title automatically delivered to your door once a month—by joining as a Friend of PM Press. And, we'll throw in a free T-shirt when you sign up.

Here are your options:

- **$30 a month** Get all books and pamphlets plus 50% discount on all webstore purchases

- **$40 a month** Get all PM Press releases (including CDs and DVDs) plus 50% discount on all webstore purchases

- **$100 a month** Superstar—Everything plus PM merchandise, free downloads, and 50% discount on all webstore purchases

For those who can't afford $30 or more a month, we have **Sustainer Rates** at $15, $10 and $5. Sustainers get a free PM Press T-shirt and a 50% discount on all purchases from our website.

Your Visa or Mastercard will be billed once a month, until you tell us to stop. Or until our efforts succeed in bringing the revolution around. Or the financial meltdown of Capital makes plastic redundant. Whichever comes first.

That Precious Strand of Jewishness That Challenges Authority

Leon Rosselson

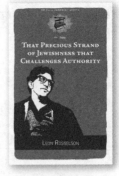

ISBN: 978-1-62963-378-7
$5.95   32 pages

"For my parents and grandparents, Jewish identity, in religion, culture and language, was a given. Not so for me. I'm not religious, not a Zionist, so in what consists my Jewishness? Is a love of chopped liver and a belief that chicken soup cures all ills enough? And does it matter? This is the story of my search for answers. It is an argument with myself, with song lyrics to embellish the argument."

Like so many of those others in Britain of Jewish lineage, songwriter and award-winning folk singer Leon Rosselson is descended from antecedents who fled pogroms in eastern Europe. Pertinently, he questions what being a Jew means—is it adherence to Judaism as a religion, an ethnicity, a citizen of Israel, or someone who eats "chicken soup with knedlach"? He describes clearly and with historical insight how any concept of "Jewishness" can involve all of those things and more. In his own life, he has decided to pick and choose from this tradition and history and build on what he deems to be the progressive, humane, and universalist values of that Jewish background.

Rosselson is a strong supporter of Palestinian rights, seeing in the victimization of Palestinians by the state of Israel parallels with historical Jewish persecution. He concludes this short essay by stating: "I share with the growing number of Jews in the diaspora who place solidarity with the oppressed above demands of tribalism and with those in Israel who dare to stand against the powers that be."

"His songs are fierce, funny, cynical, outraged, blasphemous, challenging and anarchic. And the tunes are good, too."
—*Guardian* (UK)

"With dazzling lyrical technique, deftly woven inter-rhymes, a powerful understanding of image, irony and narrative verse, he paints vivid portraits of sadly displaced lives, fools in high places, the absurdities and the occasional graces of modern life."
—*Boston Globe*

The World Turned Upside Down: Rosselsongs 1960–2010

Leon Rosselson

ISBN: 978-1-60486-498-4
UPC: 760137521624
$44.95   294 min. / 80 pages

The life and times of England's greatest living songwriter are captured in a deluxe box set, containing 72 songs on 4 CDs and an 80-page book.

"The songs on these CDs span 5 decades, from the sparky sixties to the curdled present, and encompass a wide variety of song subjects and song forms. They have been written out of hope, anger, love, scorn, laughter and despair. The tracks I have selected are, I believe, sturdily built and quite capable of standing up for themselves. And, because they have something to say about the times in which they were written, there are copious notes on the political and personal environments that formed them along with some pointed observations on the craft of songwriting." —Leon Rosselson

Where Are the Barricades? (CD)

Leon Rosselson

ISBN: 978-1-62963-219-3
UPC: 877746007521
$14.95   53 min.

Best known for his song "The World Turned Upside Down" as performed and made into a top 10 hit by Billy Bragg, Leon Rosselson has blessed us with songs for nearly six full decades. The *Guardian* has called his compositions "fierce, funny, cynical, outraged, blasphemous, challenging, and anarchic," and *Folk Roots* called him "a superb integrator of words and music." Now at 81 years old, Rosselson leaves us with his swan song and final recording, *Where Are the Barricades?* A collection of all-new songs, *Where Are the Barricades?* culminates a triumphant career, and firmly solidifies Rosselson's reputation as one of England's most prolific and respected songwriters.